Editions **HOUVET**

★

CHARTRES CATHEDRAL

★

Revised by
MALCOLM B. MILLER B.A.,
English guide of CHARTRES CATHEDRAL

★

The chapter " ARCHITECTURE "
translated by Mr. MALCOLM MILLER from a text by
JEAN VILLETTE

★

Illustrations by
E. HOUVET - FRANCESCHI - LANIEPCE

★

Printed 11-1972 by
Imprimeries Loos - Saint-Dié

ÉTIENNE HOUVET ❊ ❧

CHARTRES CATHEDRAL

*Being an Extract of a work honoured
by the Académie des Beaux-Arts*

Pythagoras (12th Century)

Editions HOUVET
20, rue de Rechèvres
CHARTRES

CONTENTS

Gothic Art.

FOREWORD
My impressions as a custodian
By Etienne HOUVET

Our Lady of Chartres is one of the finest churches raised to the Glory of God and the Virgin Mary. Its structure is solid without heaviness, its proportions perfect, its magnificent steeples like an invitation to prayer, and the severe beauty of its west façade seeming to scorn vain ornaments.

What strong emotions uplift the soul from the instant we enter the nave with its harmonious lines ! We do not, however, in any way have the impression of being crushed by the stone blocks suspended some 115 feet overhead, for massive, but elegant, piers support them, and there is about the whole building a reassuring robustness and balance.

Then one walks on as if clad in a garment of gems which fall from our unrivalled windows ; their soft light runs along the walls and floods the pavement ; the colouring changes with the season and the hour, and, of an evering, when the last rays of the setting sun creep through the transparent mosaic, it is as if the walls were strewn with golden dust.

Did some medieval magicians want to carry us away to dreamland ? No ; artists merely tried to represent what the mystic city is, in which man's soul can meet with God ; their ambition was to make of the church a dwelling worthy of the Virgin whom they worshipped.

A few steps farther will take us behind the chancel, where the vaulting in the ambulatory is a masterpiece. Now we enter a palm-forest, in which the light becomes more subdued as the only openings are the lower windows, which are darker than those of either the transepts or the clerestory.

The Christ of the Book of Revelation (12th Century)

Whether lifting our eyes to the soaring nave vaults, or peering into the depths of the aisles, the whole atmosphere is one of religious mystery, and believers and atheists alike, provided they have a receptive and sensitive mind, cannot but experience a little of that unearthly joy so keenly felt by the devotees of our cathedral.

Yet they might pass by our statuary and miss all its significance — though it serves us as an open book from which we may read the heart of the medieval sculptors.

Let the custodian therefore guide you ; and let us first study that peerless royal door, a work dating from 1150 or thereabouts. Nothing here is given to corporeal beauty ; and one is led to wonder how men — men of genius they surely were — could, in the very birth of their art, thus show the soul radiating through the body, thus open up vistas on the divine. Behold the Christ of the middle tympanum ; what stateliness and dignity in his bearing! He sits enthroned, surrounded by the elders of the Apocalypse ; they, glorious in their ecstasy ; he, regal in his triumph.

And what shall we say of those tall figures, kings and queens of Judah, the supposed ancestors of Christ ? They belong to the world beyond, and the serenity of their countenances seems to reflect beatific vision.

West Front (12th, 13th, 16th Century)

If you should be tempted to say these are but rough draughts, clumsy attempts of an immature art unable yet to master life, we should deny the charge, and urge you to take a look at other scenes. Side by side with the apocalyptic vision, labour is represented and honoured. We have done now with composure and bliss, and we find everyday acts and gestures are faithfully pictured. Here, under the allegorical figures of the liberal arts, we find those scholars who excelled in each branch of learning. What pains they seem to take! Their knotted brows and tense faces show how strenuously they work. Here, too in twelve most delightful and realistic little scenes, we watch the round of a year's toil.

The transept doors are quite different : art has come a step nearer to man. Look at the Christ of the south porch. He embodies our dream of a God *come down from heaven, the Word made flesh.* He stands in the midst of his apostles, no longer stamped with majesty but kindness seems to cloud his features ; he looks as if aware of the difficulties of his mission among men.

His church stands about him. In the bay to his right are the holy Martyrs. A pope, Saint Clement, is leanning on his crosier and personifies authority. Two deacons, Saint Stephen and Saint Lawrence, attend him with due meekness and obedience. A bishop, Saint Denis, has a deacon on his right, Saint Vincent, and on his left Saint Piat, a priest : both in a submissive attitude. The two groups are heralded by two proud knights, Saint Maurice and Saint George.

In the bay to the left of Christ, Saint Sylvester and Saint Ambrose are rigid figures, as becomes Doctors of the Church ; Saint Nicholas, with his wonted kindness, has a gesture of blessing ; and the apostle of Gaul, Saint Martin, is full of grandeur and dignity. Near him, we notice Saint Jerome holding a Bible ; no doubt the artist deliberately gave him that austere look to remind us of his long fasting in the desert and his arduous study of the Holy Scriptures. On the extreme left and right are two meditating monks, Saint Laumer and Saint Avitus.

Here we are no longer facing immaterial, impersonal creatures, but man wholly revealed through his acts with his own individuality.

Let us walk to the North porch, with its scenes from the Old Testament. Here stand the prophets, grim and stern, their faces reflecting their inner thoughts, the coming of Christ the Saviour.

Two figures especially draw our attention. We behold a John

the Baptist, his body emaciated through long penance, and a face on which deep sorrow is written : he feels crushed under the weight of the sinful world his master has come to redeem. And what of Saint Modesta ? Virginal beauty irradiates through all her person, at once so demure and so stately.

Scenes there are here in which the old masters expressed their whole soul : those, for instance, of the Virgin's death and resurrection. What peace on her face ! and how infinite the respect with which the angels approach the tomb of their Queen and lay hands on her shroud !

Again we are seized with admiration by the Creation of the World. With a wave of his arm, God brings Heaven and Earth out of Chaos. Higher up, after having divided the light from the darkness, He is lost in meditation ! Could any seer penetrate his thoughts ? He is about to create Adam : a masterpiece ! With what love and tenderness he shapes the first man *in his image, after his likeness*. Then comes the scene of temptation, followed by the fall, and the Almighty shows a face of wrath : He will punish, and drive the guilty pair out of Eden.

Another cycle of labour is carved in this porch far less damaged by the elements than that on the west front and for the second time we feel the charm of these life-like scenes. How familiar to us is the mower starting for the field in June ! And how realistic the sower who, in October, sows his seed ! Yet most delightful of all the rustic who, shivering with cold, and may be just come in from a snowstorm, takes off his shoes before the hearth.

This is but a short record of our impressions. To guide the tourist in his study of the wonderful cathedral, we think it might be well to give him :

1° A history of the building ;
2° Architecture ;
3° A description of the royal portal ;
4° A description of the north porch ;
5° A description of the south porch ;
6° A description of the choir enclosure screen ;
7° A description of the windows.

May these few lines, written by a sincere admirer of the cathedral inspire in all lovers of the Middle Ages the desire to visit it more frequently and more completely.

THE PILGRIMAGE

Chartres, one of the " high places of Christendom ", was the cradle, and, up to this day, has remained the sanctuary of a pilgrimage that is one of the most ancient and famous. The list of our bishops, dating back to the 4th. century A. D., indicates that since that time there has been an important church here.

The biography of Saint Béthaire, the bishop of Chartres in the last years of the 6th century, — very likely written in the 9th century and based on local scripts, tells us one day... " the holy man was kneeling before an altar of the blessed Virgin Mary "[1].

We may therefore assume the Virgin had an altar in the 6th century church.

A manuscript of the 8th century mentions a donation of King Pépin (in 768) to the Abbey of Saint-Denis, " with the exception of what had previously been given to other various churches, particularly to Saint-Mary's church in Chartres "[2], from which we conclude the 8th century church was already dedicated to the Virgin.

Owing to the long and ever-growing renown of the worship of Mary, our church received from King Charles the Bald the tunic or veil of the Virgin.

Our chronicle records how, in 911, bishop Gantelme unfolded the holy relic at the New Gate, while Rollon and his Normans were besieging the town. They were immediately put to flight.

In 1194 the relic was thought to have been lost in the fire which destroyed much of the town. At first there was hesitation whether or not to rebuild the church, but after four days the precious tunic was unearthed, and the reconstruction was decided upon with great enthusiasm.

---

1. DUCHESNE, " *Episcopal records of ancient Gaul vol. II, page 423.*
2. FELIBIEN, " *A history of the Royal Abbey of Saint-Denis* " p. XXX.
   Chartulary of Our Lady of Chartres, I, p. 70.

Chartres was then what Lourdes is today. Sick people were nursed in the crypt, generally for a period of nine days.

The veneration of Our Lady drew great crowds here. The pilgrims slept in the cathedral, which accounts for the slope of the nave paving allowing a thorough washing, and panels of the stained-glass windows could be taken out to air the building.

Our Lady was bountiful in dealing with her pilgrims. A Latin document of the first years of the 13th century, kept in the library of the Vatican, relates miracles that took place in our city, beloved of Mary, and considerably helped to spread the reputation of the sanctuary, even beyond the frontiers.

A French translation of the Latin text by Jean Le Marchand (destroyed in 1944 by an air-raid) extols the liberality of the faithful, who dragged the stones necessary for the reconstruction as well as the many and diverse gifts ranging from the richest jewels to the daily food destined for the workers. One of our 13th century windows illustrates the fact.

In the course of the 12th century, three popes visited Chartres, and numerous were the saints that prayed here..., Saint-Bernard, the abbot of Clairvaux, Saint-Thomas of Canterbury, saint François de Sales, saint Vincent de Paul, saint Louis-Marie Grignon de Monfort, in the 17th; and, more recently, saint Benoit Labre.

Many of our kings came as pilgrims ; and some offered magnificents gifts. The North Rose was given by Blanche de Castille and Saint Louis. Henry III, a frequent visitor — he came about twenty times, — often prolonged his stay in our town. Henri IV was consecrated here. This royal patronage proved beneficial both to the cathedral and the city.

In about 1510, to give satisfaction to the people's devotion, a statue of Our Lady was placed before the screen.

The 16th century saw many important pilgrimages, of which we shall only mention the so-called white pilgrimage, when more than twenty thousand people walked from Dreux.

During the Revolution, the Holy Relic was desecrated and partly lost. The very ancient statue of Our Lady of the Crypt was burnt in front of the church in December 1793.

The cathedral was then used as a temple to the Goddess Reason, and strange ceremonies were performed in the worship of the Supreme Being.

Though mutilated at that time, the building was saved from the complete destruction which had been planned at first.

It was only gradually given back to its former and rightful use. The chief altar in the crypt was not consecrated before 1855 ; and, in the same year, the statue, henceforth known as Our Lady of the Pillar was placed where it is now : both events coinciding with the promulgation of the dogma of the Immaculate Conception.

In 1857, a new statue was carved for the crypt, from drawings of the most venerated image burnt by the Revolution.

The year 1893 saw a national pilgrimage ; and 1876, a jubilee for the millennial anniversary : religious manifestations that brought great crowds here.

In 1890, the diocesan pilgrimage was instituted.

The crypt is the origin and heart of the pilgrimage. For many centuries Our Lady of Chartres has accepted the homage of her votaries. Our Lady of the " Belle Verrière " was once an object of veneration, and particularly invoked by women before childbirth, and formerly, there was the gilt statue on the main altar, where people knelt in prayer as to-day before Our Lady of the Pillar.

Among the statues which were lost, we must mention : Notre-Dame-la-Blanche, placed before the screen in the 14th century ; a seated virgin of gilt silver that was in the chancel, on the main altar. When people came to kneel before her and pray, they interrupted the celebration of the canons' office, the reason why Our Lady of the Pillar was carved. Lastly, Our Lady of the Crypt, burnt by the revolutionaries in 1793, was replaced by a copy in 1857.

The Virgin of the Crypt

The Crypt (11th Century)

Many contemporary writers were devoted pilgrims to Our Lady of Chartres. Huysmans has described, in the graphic manner which is his, morning mass in the crypt. Psichari, after his conversion, came by way of thanksgiving for his first holy communion. Péguy tramped the roads of Beauce, gazing at the old spire, '' without its equal in the world ''. René Schwob, converted, found in the Royal Doorway the title and subject of a fine book, for which he stayed in Chartres on two different occasions.

All these men and others, still living, have shown the way to the younger generation.

Pilgrimages are now reviving. Groups of people cross each other's path in the cathedral : parishioners, novices, seminaries, groups of the ,, Action Catholique '', scouts, students. Concerning the latter, let us mention their traditional pilgrimage each spring. In 1936, when it began, it counted about fifteen pilgrims ; nowadays they are many thousands of young people. Following the medieval tradition, they walk half the way, heavily laden, meditating, praying and singing. Who can measure the radiating influence of such proceeding at a time when, much more than in the 13th century, we need " lodgers for our God and Our Lady " ?

Our Lady of the Pillar (16th Century)
Cl. Franceschi

A HISTORY OF THE CATHEDRAL

The first church dated from no later than the 4th century. It stood at the foot of the gallo-roman wall and was burnt in 743 by a Duke of Aquitaine. The second also was burnt, in 858 by Danish pirates.

Bishop Gislebert at once began the work of reconstruction and expansion. From this church only the martyrium is left, known today as the Saint Lubin Chapel. It was lit by five windows, now walled in. This church in its turn was destroyed by fire during the night of 7th September 1020.

Saint Fulbert was then bishop of Chartres. All of the great prelate's genius, science and piety went into the building of the new church. To his letters, King Robert and other sovereigns of Europe, including King Carnute, responded by sending magnificent gifts. Fulbert began with the crypt ; and, round the martyrium, he had an ambulatory built, opening into three large barrel-vaulted chapels, and extending on either side into galleries. He then built an upper church : in length 108 metres, and in width : 34 metres.

The fire which burnt the town in 1134 damaged the front of the church as well as the bell-tower. It was then that the north tower was begun, to be completed about 1150. It consisted only of two stories and had a lead-covered roof. The south tower was begun in about 1144 and was completed, with its spire, about 1160, and is certainly one of the finest steeples in the world. The harmony of its proportions is exquisite, and the architect who designed it showed remarkable skill in the way he contrived to pass from the square tower to the octagonal spire, rising towards heaven with such slenderness and majesty. The total height is 105 metres.

The Royal Portal was built in the middle of the 12th century, probably between 1145 and 1155.

During the night of June 10. 1194, Fulbert's renowned church burnt, the flames sparing only the crypt, the towers and the newly-built façade.

This was a great catastrophe in Christendom, for the pilgrimage to the Virgin of Chartres was one of the most popular.

The pope's legate happened to be in Chartres at the time. He gathered together the clergy and the people, and roused such enthusiasm that, forgetting private losses, one and all vowed they would raise a new and even more splendid church. Bishop Regnault de Mouçon and the canons relinquished their prebends for three years. Following such notable example, the people brought large offerings. Kings and nobles proved no less magnificent : all classes shared in rebuilding the cathedral. The work, under the control of an unknown master, went forward with great rapidity. The church, begun in 1194, was roofed in 1220 : and this accounts for the unity of style which is unmistakable throughout.

The cathedral, as it now stands, with its architecture, glass and sculpture, but with its seven steeples left unfinished, was almost completed within only 25 years, although it was not reconsecrated until October 1260.

Most archeologists are agreed that after the crypts had been consolidated and transformed, the rebuilding of the cathedral was undertaken in three principal efforts :

1° The nave, aisles, and lower parts of the transepts.

2° The choir, and apsidal chapels.

3° The upper parts of the transepts.

A rood screen formerly closed the entrance to the choir. During the second half of the 13th century, a third section was added to the north tower slightly higher than the west rose.

Minor work went on afterwards. — The vestry was built in the last quarter of the century. In 1326 a fine chapel was raised close to the apse, and dedicated to Saint Piat, whose relics used to draw crowds of pilgrims. This chapel, which measures 15 metres 40 in length and 7 metres 20 in width divided into four bays, is very pure in style and harmonious in its proportions. The capitals and bosses denote perfect craftsmanship and the fourteenth century glass affords great interest. Note a fine double piscina unfortunately damaged.

In 1413, Louis of Bourbon, Count of Vendôme, then a prisoner, vowed that, should he be released, he would raise a chapel to Our Lady. In 1417 he had a chapel opened in the fifth bay of the southern aisle, which still bears his name, but which, built in the flamboyant style of the period, is out of keeping with the rest of the building.

In 1507, Jean Texier began the new spire, which he completed in 1513. In the following year he began work on the choir-screen.

It was in 1753 that the canons started their devastating campaign in the choir. They completely covered the pillars with vulgar-looking stucco, and replaced the tapestries hanging behind the stalls by marble reliefs. Bridan was commissioned to sculpt the Assumption group for the main altar.

In 1836, the carelessness of a work-man caused another dreadful conflagration. The roof and the two belfreys were entirely burnt and the bells melted ; yet the building itself was not harmed and the glass was untouched. An iron roof covered with copper plates has taken the place of the once famous timber forest.

The Ambulatory and South Aisle (13th Century)

ARCHITECTURE

The place of Chartres Cathedral in the

History of Architecture

From romanesque architecture Chartres Cathedral has retained strength and purity of mass, to which is added the vertical thrust dear to the whole gothic period.

The unknown master who conceived it before the end of the 12th century introduced innovations which henceforth were to direct the art of building. He thrust up ogival vaults to a height never before attained, and surpassed in few other edifices, persuaded that he was able to counter their formidable pressure almost exclusively by the use of flying-butresses. A justified prudence incited him nevertheless to add further butressing concealed beneath the roofing of the aisles, a formula he inherited from his predecessors. But he had the audacity to abandon the expedient of a tribune, the function of which in the great churches started earlier, was to act as a shoulder to the main body of the building.

Almost all architects were henceforth to be inspired by the construction experimented at Chartres. Amiens and Reims, the most representative cathedrals in the French style of the 13th century, were modelled upon Chartres, applying its essential principles, but going further still in the direction of lightness and luminosity.

Their builders could do this, especially as they were unrestricted, unlike the master of Chartres, who had to construct over the crypt built in the first quarter of the 11th century by the bishop Saint Fulbert, and which survived the fire of 1194. These solid foundations, about 30 feet in depth, together with those of earlier edifices, were to support the new cathedral, imposing their form upon it to the extent of determining its width and the disposition of the apsidal chapels. The Royal façade, which, with its towers, also survived the fire, served as the western limit. It remained to mount above the three romanesque windows the section containing the great rose. Only the long transept was free to overlap the old plan. No longer quadripartite as in Laon Cathedral, the interior elevation of Chartres was divided into three as in Notre-Dame de Paris, but with the fundamental difference that the vast tribunes gave way to a triforium which ran the length of the top of the aisles. These consequently are lighter. A new path was hereby opened up, and appeared again at much the same time in the choir of Soissons Cathedral.

The plan of Notre-Dame de Chartres has several unique characteristics. The main body of the building, adapted to the foundations of the earlier romanesque church, attains the width of 16.40 meters between the axes of the piers. The nave itself corresponds in width to the three bays of the façade together, and is flanked by single aisles, as later in Reims, whilst around the choir they are doubled, as in Notre-Dame de Paris and later in Amiens. From the double ambulatory seven apsidal chapels open up, of which three, more developed, are built over the chapels of the 11th century crypt. The transept crosses at quite a distance from the chevet of the cathedral, as in Paris, and gives an exceptional length to the choir, which is only slightly shorter than that of Laon. Of all French churches the choir of Chartres is the vastest, and the total area of the cathedral is only surpassed by that of Amiens, which was augmented later by side chapels. As for the transept, still larger than that of Laon it is aisled, as at Laon, Amiens, Reims, and Beauvais.

Whereas a fine-grained stone was used for the sculpture of the porches, for the building itself the masons, as in the past, exploited the quarries of Berchères, five miles from Chartres. These provided, and indeed continue to do so, an admirable hard calcous stone, one of the fines available, both for its tone and for its resistance to soiling and disintegration.

The crypt

Any visit desirous of proceeding chronologically should start with the substructure. The Saint-Lubin crypt, constructed in the 9th century, and interred deeply beneath the choir, is built against

The Ambulatory (13th Century)

the wall of an even older edifice. Beneath the choir is the oldest part of the cathedral, known as the Saint Lubin crypt, built in the 9th century. A second and much larger crypt, the Saint Fulbert Crypt was built between 1020 and 1024, and embraces the remains of the carolingian church. Its galleries extend beneath the aisles and the chevet of the present cathedral. Of all the ancient crypts of France this is the most extensive, and is only surpassed in area by those of Saint Peter's in Rome, and Canterbury Cathedral. Groin-vaulting is found throughout, except in the ambulatory, where there are three chapels with barrel-vaulting, and between these, are four more chapels with powerful ogival vaulting, added to Fulbert's construction when the building of the present cathedral was undertaken. Besides the interest of its architecture, the crypt is notable for a 12th century mural painting, for the well of the Saints-Forts, rich in both history and legend, and dating from the gallo-roman oppidum, and also for the shrine of Our Lady of the Crypt. Here a statue of the Virgin, sculpted in the 19th century, replaces the wooden image of the romanesque period burnt during the French Revolution.

The two galleries of the crypt were each lengthened one bay in the 12th century in order to link them with the stairs leading down from ground level under the towers. At the foot of the south stair is a baptismal font of the same period. In the chapel of Saint Martin several column-statues, originally from the Royal Portal, may be seen, together with the famous Sun-dial Angel. They were placed here in order to protect them from further disintegration.

Exterior of the Cathedral

Emerging from the crypts on the south side, we are in an ideal position to contemplate the Old Spire. This was completed in one effort starting in 1145, and originally towered over a structure less elevated than that of the 13th century. From this angle it appears less part of the neighbouring mass. In it a perfect transition is effected from the square tower base to the octagonal spire. The upward movement of the butresses is continued through the columns of the pinnacles, and the ribs of the spire itself are suggested as from the last square section of the tower with the short tapered forms at the corners beneath the pinnacles. The pointed gables accentuate the upward movement, as do the four pyramids which counter the weight of the immense stone spire, the highest of its kind. Without the aid of any timberwork, it is composed of flat sides which narrow progressively towards the pinnacle, and is a prodigy of lightness and audacity, an expression of strength and purity never attained to such a degree.

Near the base of the butresses on the south side of this spire is a curious piece of sculpture known as the " Ass playing a viol ", and beside it is the Sundial Angel, which comes from the same work-shop as the column-statues of the Royal Portal.

The principal façade, for the most part, is virtually none other than the ancient façade preserved from the romanesque cathedral. The North Tower, elder sister of the Old Spire, in its lower stages at least, differs little from it. In the centre of this deliberately sobre ensemble is the Royal Portal with its rich sculpture accumulated in a restricted space, and linked strongly with the three windows which surmount it. The section in which the great rose blossoms was added during the reconstruction work of the 13th century, and replaced the 12th century pinnacle. This rose, one of the most ancient known, is remarkable for its stone work, best seen from the outside.

It was in the second half of the 13th century that the gallery of kings was added, as well as the large square base, later transformed, which supports the North steeple. The timber and lead steeple which stood there earlier was often struck by lightning, and was replaced after the fire of July 26th 1506 by the stone steeple which Jean Texier, known as Jean de Beauce, conceived and executed with such dexterity. Realised between 1507 and 1513, its structure, both masterly and simple, is guessed at under the exuberance of its flamboyant decoration, in which the Renaissance is discreetly manifest.

The value of some architectural ensembles is to be found in their unity. Others such as the façade of Chartres Cathedral are animated by the contrasts in them, and reflect at the same time changes in form over the centuries.

At the foot of the North Tower is a small pavillion which shelters the mechanism of a clock, constructed in 1520 in the Renaissance style by the same Jean de Beauce. The richly polychromed face, around which the finger turns in a 24 hour cycle, is more than 18 feet in diameter. In the base is cut a tiny charming door of the 13th century.

The nave butresses carry the abutments of the flying butresses.

Nave flying-butresses (13th Century)

These, recognised as the most ancient that can be given the name, are composed of a double arch powerfully reinforced by small columns which remind one of the spokes of a wheel. Each of these columns, with its base and its capital, is hewn from one block of stone. The upper arches, which had not been part of the original plan, were added later, and lean against the sort of pyramids, destined to serve as pinnacles in the earlier plan. A single niche sheltering a statue decorates each abutment, whose sobriety is indicative of their functional nature. The projection of successive butresses expresses in a most striking way the forces that are involved and which are canalized down from the soaring vaults to the ground.

A cornice runs along the top of the walls of the cathedral, forming a gallery along which one may walk, and through the abutments of the upper butresses openings are cut through which one may pass. Beneath the two sets of flying-butresses are huge columns which alternate, circular, octagonal, from bay to bay.

The north rose, with eight lancet windows cut deeply in the corners beneath it, is decorated above by sculptured figures. The triple porch beneath is surmounted by a sharply defined stone roof supported by sets of complex outer pillar combinations with statues similar to those decorating the inner porches. The gable above the rose is flanked by towers constructed in place of the originally intended flying-butresses; the severity of their butresses relieved somewhat by the little constructions with their columns and pediments, which are linked with the abutments of the choir and the apse.

A flying buttress of the choir (13th Century)

Near the North Porch is the sacristy, built during the second half of the 13th century, and lit by elegant windows with mullions and cusps.

A Louis XV iron gate gives access to the garden and the old bishop's palace, with its brick and stone work, characteristics of the beginning of the 17th century. The garden and the terrace afford many different views of the cathedral, especially of the chevet with its chapels set upon those of the crypt beneath. Among the latter, the most prominent, those of the 11th century, were reinforced with a second thickness of wall when the present cathedral was begun, and at the same time four chapels were opened up between them. As a result of the different widths of the 11th and the 13th century chapels, the flying-butresses also had to be placed at differing intervals.

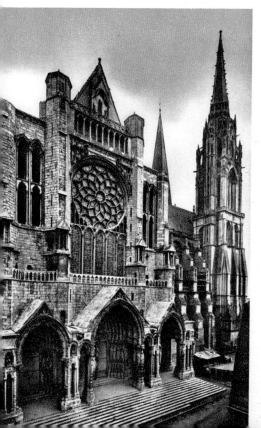

*The North Porch
(13th Century)*

These flying-butresses are disposed in much the same way as those of the nave, but they were built without underpropping, and their small prismatic pillars, having neither base nor capitals, take the place of proper columns. Above all, and this is their essential difference, they project out over the second ambulatory, and as the thrusts are thus distributed onto double butresses, these are lighter and more slender than those of the nave.

The bronze angel on the roof of the chevet pivots on ball-bearings and indicates the wind direction. It replaces the angel of the Middle Ages, which melted during the fire which destroyed the roof timbers in 1836. It was following this disaster that the present metal framework was put into place and covered with a copper roof, since turned green through oxydation.

Behind the apse is the chapel of Saint Piat, the flat chevet of which is flanked by two cylindrical towers. It is lit by vast windows with stained glass for the most part from the 14th century, as in fact is the whole construction. The ground floor room was originally a chapter house. A charming open staircase links the upper chapel with the cathedral.

The façade of the south transept differs in many ways from that of the north. The rose and the lancets here are cut into a plain wall. Slender columns run up the butresses, strengthening them and at the same time giving an impression of great lightness. The two towers have high twin bays opened up in their lateral faces. The porch is covered by pinnacles in which statues are set, and its forward pillars display sculpture in high relief on all four sides.

Set between two of the nave butresses about 1413 is the Vendôme chapel, an interesting example of flamboyant style, with a window surmounted by a gable, and statury characterised by the hip movement in favour at the time.

The two apse towers, the four of the transept, and that of the crossing, hidden under the roof, were intended to support spires, which were never built. This original plan is not at all evident, and its abandon is fortunate, for such a bristling of spires would only have detracted from the two whose silhouette stand out from afar against the sky of Beauce.

The interior

On entering the cathedral by the Royal Porch, a vivid impression, accentuated by the light from the stained-glass, is produced by the amplitude of the building. On either side of this entrance are rooms beneath the towers with ogival vaulting, which, still in the romanesque tradition, fall onto the capitals of the columns whose bases are ornamented with claw shapes. From these rooms one has a good view of the nave through openings which originally linked them with the narthex. The vaults of this narthex used to support a tribune, traces of which can be seen on the walls of the towers, and two columns of which still exist against the wall on either side beneath the 12th century windows. The ogival vaults of the two bays between the towers fall onto groups of columns grafted onto the older tower walls. This part of the edifice still shows traces of reconstruction work done in the 16th century.

The South Porch (13th Century)

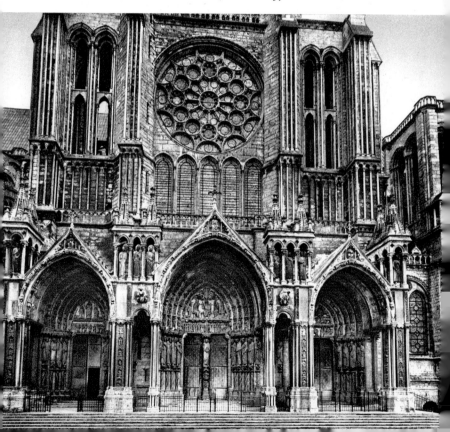

The nave, built after the fire of 1194, is joined to the towers by massive columns. The cathedral, one of the earliest churches to have vaults which form the diagonals of a rectangle instead of a square, reposes on pillars which differ only in that they are alternatively round and octagonal. Above the triforium, in each bay, are double lancets divided by a prismatic mullion, and surmounted by cusped rose windows. Whilst in the towers, which are still predominantly romanesque, the broken arch is widely used, in the 13th century parts, except in the apse, the arches are semi-circular.

The paving slopes. This was, originally, to facilitate the cleaning by water after the passing of pilgrims who slept in the church in the Middle Ages. In the centre of the nave is the labyrinth, whose meandering path, symbolising the Way of the Cross, was followed by penitents.

One doubtlessly notices the absence of tombs in the cathedral. This is deliberate, and is out of respect for the Virgin's divine privilege at Her death, the cathedral itself being consecrated " The cathedral-church of Our Lady of the Assumption ".

At the transept crossing, as near the towers, multiple columns spring up to the vault.

On comparing the three rose windows, an evolution will be noticed from the West, in which the stone-work plays an important role, to the North, where there is a predominance of glass filled spaces.

Whilst admitting that the high altar, by Bridan, is a work of considerable merit, it must be regretted that the 18th century found it necessary to cover the architecture of the choir with marble and stucco, destroying thereby the rythm which linked it with the nave.

In the double aisle of the choir the piers are single, except those which support the weight of the chevet towers above. Around the choir is a screen of the 16th century, which brings to this part of the cathedral a note of exuberance and preciosity. In the ambulatory admirable views open up, composed of chapels, irregularly-spaced piers, and an interplay of vaults, which, with the stained glass, create effects not to be encountered elsewhere.

Although each era has brought its contribution to it, the Cathedral of Chartres remains, nevertheless, one of the most homogeneous architectural creations to have come down to us from the Middle Ages.

Cl. Franceschi

Here are the principal dimensions of Chartres Cathedral :

Total length 135 m 98.
Outside width of the nave 44 m 03.
Outside width of the transept 73 m 40 including porches.
Outside width of the choir 53 m 30.
Distance between the piers 7 m 08.
Span accross the nave 16 m 42.
Internal width of the nave between walls 32 m 20.
Internal width across transept 61 m 80 by 28 m 08.
Internal width across the choir 45 m 90.
Height from transept paving to top of boss 35 m.
Height to clerestory sill 20 m 50.
Height to triforium paving 15 m 60.
Height from base of the South tower to point of steeple 102 m 64.
Height from base of North tower to point of steeple 111 m 44.
Diameter of West Rose 15 m 42.
Diameter of the labyrinth 12 m 91.
Length of walk around labyrinth 262 m 60.
Orientation of the cathedral 46° 54' 30'' E of geographic N.

Transept crossing

Royal Door (12th Century)

THE WEST OR ROYAL PORTAL [1]

TWELFTH CENTURY

Until recently it was believed that this mid-12th. century portal had originally stood further back behind the towers, and was moved forwards after the 1194 fire, but recent research has shown that, on the contrary, it was constructed in its present position, although the sculpture was probably intended for an inner narthex door which was not built, and then hurriedly adapted to the outer position.

---

1. The name of " Royal Portal " very likely goes as far back as the time of its erection. Ms 1058 of the Municipal Library in Chartres gives material proof it was used in the first decades of the thirteenth century.

The three doors, which open directly into the nave, are decorated with a well-ordered sculptural programme. The right bay represents the descent of Christ to our world, the left, His ascension, while in the central tympanum He is seen apocalyptically on His second coming. Those events in Christ's life related to His birth and death, the Incarnation, and the Passion and the Resurrection cycles, are sculpted on the frieze, made up of almost 200 small figures.

The subject matter of these scenes is taken from both the New Testament and the Apocryphal Gospels, and do not follow in chronological order. The story begins on the left of the central door, and reads to the left as far as the North Tower, then continues on the right of the central door, and reads to the right as far as the South Tower.

1. Joachim and Anne are spurned by the high priest because they are childless.

2. They go away, grieving.

3. Joachim among his flocks, is visited by an angel.

4. He meets his wife at the Golden Gate.

5. Mary is born and washed in a tub by two women.

6. Joachim and Anne bring their young child to the temple.

7. The three are seen journeying together.

8. Mary climbs the steps, while her father stands by and her mother is seated.

9. The parents return home.

10. Mary is taken to the altar by the high priest and Saint Joseph who holds a flowering stem.

11. Joseph and Mary join hands before the high priest who is marrying them.

12. They go to Nazareth.

13. Mary and Joachim are seated. To the left an angel announces the birth of Christ.

14. Mary visits her cousin Elisabeth and wonders, seeing her with child.

15. The Nativity. Jesus is lying on his mother's bed. Saint Joseph is seated, and the two midwives, Zelemi and Salome, stand near by, ready to help. The ox is seen in the background.

16. Angels announce the good tidings to the shepherds.

17. The Wise Men inquire of Herod the birthplace of the new king of the Jews.

18. They bring their offerings to Jesus. Servants hold the horses.

19. The flight into Egypt.

20. The Massacre of the Innocents. A soldier brings a mother and her son to Herod, who sits, sword drawn, on his throne. Another soldier wields a sabre, and a third dashes out the brains of a helpless child.

21. Jesus among the doctors.

22. The Circumcision.

23. The Presentation of Jesus at the temple.

24. The journey to Jerusalem.

25. The return to Nazareth.

26. The Baptism of Christ. The Jordan is shown by waving lines.

27. The temptation in the wilderness.

28. Judas is prompted by two Jewish priests to sell his master.

29. The Last Supper.

30. The Betrayal. Kissed by Judas, Jesus is led away, while Peter cuts off the ear of Malchus.

31. The Entry into Jerusalem.

32. The Entombment of Jesus.

33. The Holy Women, coming to the sepulchre, find it empty ; the soldiers set to watch sleep.

34. Jesus washing the apostles' feet.

35. He walks with the two disciples from Emmaus.

36. The meal at Emmaus.

37. The disciples return to Jerusalem in order to tell what they have seen.

38. Christ's apparition to Saint Thomas.

I. - Right Door

On the lower lintel, we see, to the left :

The Annunciation. Both the archangel Gabriel and the Virgin Mary are standing ; between them, an open book lies on the ground.

The Visitation, a scene in which Mary wears a royal crown.

In the middle :

The Nativity of Our Lord. The Virgin lies on a low bed ; above her is the Child, in a cradle, placed as though sacrificially upon an altar, and Saint Joseph, standing at the head of the bed, seems rapt in contemplation of the newborn babe.

To the right :

An Angel, with tidings of the Saviour's birth, appears to the shepherds, one of whom plays on his pipes, with sheep grazing at his feet.

The Annunciation to the shepherds
(12th Century)

On the upper lintel, we have another Presentation at the Temple ; to the right and left, kinsfolk bring their offerings ; in the centre, the Child is supported on the altar by his mother and Simeon.

In the tympanum the Virgin is seated with the child on her lap, a position common in Byzantine art ; on each side, an angel swings a censer. The statue is probably the one mentioned in the cartulary of the cathedral as a gift of archdeacon Richer, who died in 1150.

In the archivolts, at the bottom of the inner order, on the left, are two signs of the Zodiac : Pisces and Gemini. This inner order also contains six angels surrounding the throne of the

Virgin. The rest of the two archivolts represents the seven liberal arts, the *trivium* and the *quadrivium*, depicted in a twofold way : allegorically by women ; and historically by the seven men who were considered, each in his own way, the outstanding exponents of each art. They can be identified with some degree of certainty.

Beginning from the left, in the outer order :

1. Aristotle and Dialectic.

2. Cicero and Rhetoric.

3. Euclid and Geometry.

4. Arithmetic and either Bœthius or Pythagoras.

5. Astronomy and Ptolemy.

6. Grammar and Priscian or Donatus.

7. Music and Pythagoras, in the inner archivolt, bottom right.

The Virgin enthroned (12th Century)

II. - Left Door

In the tympanum, Christ, standing on a cloud, supported by two angels.

Below, on the lintel, four other angels lean towards the apostles, as if to say : " Ye men of Galilee, why stand ye gazing up into heaven ? This same Jesus, which is taken up from you into heaven, shall so come in like manner as ye have seen him go into heaven " (Acts I. II).

In the archivolts, the labours of the months alternate with the signs of the Zodiac. Beginning in the inner archivolt bottom right :

1. January, with his two heads symbolising the new and the old year.

2. Capricorn.

3. February, hooded, warms himself before a fire.

4. Aquarius.

5. March prunes his vine.

To the left, bottom of the inner archivolt :

1. April holds, in both hands, the branches of a tree covered with blossoms and leaves.

2. Aries.

3. May, a falconer stands near his horse, a falcon on his arm.

4. Taurus.

5. June mows his hay.

Now the outer archivolt beginning bottom left :

1. July, a harvester, cuts corn with a sickle.

2. Cancer.

3. August unties a sheaf of corn : his flail is seen behind him.

4. Leo.

5. September. A man treads grapes, while another empties a basket into the tub.

6. Virgo.

In the outer archivolt, bottom right :

1. October knocks down acorns.

2. Libra. A woman's figure that formerly held scales.

3. November slaughters his pig.

4. Scorpio

5. A man and a woman sit at a well-provided table.

6. Sagittarius.

III. - Central Doorway

We have here a " Majestas Domini " according to the Apocalypse.

In the tympanum, the figure of Christ, seated on a throne, is

Biblical figures (12th Century)

Biblical figures (12th Century)

surrounded by an oval glory ; behind his head is the cruciform nimbus, his right hand is raised in blessing, while his left holds a book resting upright on his knee. On either side, are the four beasts symbolising the four evangelists.

On the lintel below are the twelve apostles, seated in groups of three, and, at each end, an unknown figure, standing.

In the inner archivolt are twelve angels, and in the second and third, the twenty-four elders of the Apocalypse holding musical instruments and vials of perfume.

Beneath these scenes, and the capitals, stand a series of column-statues, whose identity is not known with certainty. However, according to M. Mâle[1], they would seem to represent men and women of the Old Testament, prefiguring the Old Law, and preparing for the New. M. Mâle sees Moses in the figure on the right of the left door ; Solomon, in the king holding a scroll[2] (the outer figure on the right of the central door) ; and the Queen of Sheba in the woman next to Solomon.

The twelfth century artist gave no thought to the body ; his highest ambition was to concentrate all the life of this statues in the faces. At Chartres, we can say he fully succeeded. It is impossible not to admire the look of inward joy and utmost bliss on every countenance.

In their book on " *The Sculptures of Chartres Cathedral* " Margaret and Ernest Marriage wrote : " This statuary is perhaps the most interesting thing at Chartres, and represents the art of the twelfth century at its height. "

1. L'Art Religieux au XIIe siècle en France.

2. The same king is seen on the southern doorway at Le Mans cathedral ; and the word Salomo could still be read on the scroll in 1841.

Melchizadech, Abraham, Moses, Samuel or Aaron, David (13th Century)

NORTH PORCH

THIRTEENTH CENTURY

The north porch was constructed at the beginning of the 13th century. The projecting porch was probably built with the inner portal, but a little later than the south porch. Its measurements are 33.20 meters in length, and 8.00 in depth.

Like the south porch, it consists of three bays with pointed arches surmounted with gables, corresponding to the three inner doors. The decoration, on the same general lines as that of the south, is even richer here. The vaulting of the porch is not plain but covered with bas-relief and divided by two ribs, those of the central bay being adorned with statuettes.

The north porch evokes the Old Testament, and glorifies the Virgin. It prophesises, prefigures, and prepares for Christ.

I. - Central Bay

On the central pier or trumeau, Saint Anne carries the Virgin in her arms. Beneath, Joachim kept his flocks.

On either side stand a series of statues, priests, patriarchs, and prophets, prefigurations of Christ. " These are among the most extraordinary statues of the middle ages. One feels as if they belonged to another and a higher order of men. They look as if they had been shaped of primeval clay, as if they had witnessed the dawn of the world... These patriarchs and prophets really stand for the fathers of nations, the very columns of mankind[1]. "

---

1. Emile MALE : L'Art Religieux au XIIIᵉ s.

Starting with the outer left figure :

1. Melchizedek, wearing a tiara and holding the bread and wine, the symbols of the Eucharist. According to the hundred and tenth Psalm, he is preeminently the figure of Christ. Under his feet is the Lamb.

2. Abraham, looking up at an angel, is about to sacrifice Isaac, feet tied, to be sacrificed by his father like Christ. Beneath his feet, the ram.

3. Moses, the giver of the Law, lifting up the brazen serpent, which is a symbol for Christ on the cross. John 3. 14 : '' As Moses lifted up the brazen serpent, even so must the Son of Man be lifted up. '' Beneath his feet, the golden calf.

4. Samuel, wearing the shimla, sacrifices a lamb, the symbol for Christ, the sacrifice.

5. David, as king, carries the instruments of the Passion, which he foretold in Psalm 22. Beneath him, the lion of Judah.

To the right of Saint Anne are :

6. Isaiah, the prophet of the Incarnation who foretold there should '' come forth a rod out of the stem of Jesse ''. He holds the flowering stem in his left hand, and, below him, is Jesse.

7. Jeremiah, prophet of the Passion, carrying a Greek cross.

8. Simeon, the old priest to whom Mary presented her child at the temple, holds the infant Jesus upon his arm.

9. John the Baptist clothed with camel's hair, his body wasted through long fasting. His right hand points at the Agnus Dei, the symbolised sacrifice of his cousin Christ. Beneath, a dragon.

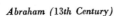
Abraham (13th Century)

John the Baptist (13th century)

We have already spoken of this extraordinary figure.

10. Saint Peter, his chalice broken, the link between the Old Testament and the New, stands dressed as Pope on the rock of the Church opposite Melchizadek. He holds the keys to Heaven and the pastoral staff.

Near Melchizadek, between the left and the central bays, is a statue of Elisha. Under him, the Shunammite woman holding a scroll.

Near Saint Peter, between the central and the right bays, Elijah stands on the wheels of his chariot. Beneath, Elisha holds his mantle.

On the lintel is the Virgin's Dormition and Resurrection. On the left side Mary reclines, her face serene. The twelve apostles are grouped around her, and Jesus receives her soul. On the right side angels translate her body gently to Heaven.

The tympanum represents her triumph. Here she is crowned and seated on a heavenly throne beside Jesus who blesses her. Above, two angels swing censers, and on each side, an angel kneels.

The inner archivolt contains twelve angels.

In the next four archivolts an imposing tree of Jesse, composed of two rows of statuettes, is flanked, by two rows of prophets.

The seventh and eighth orders, contain fourty-four statuettes of seated figures holding scrolls and books.

The decoration of the outer arch is consecrated to the story of the Creation and the Fall. On the very outside, with one exception, are figures of God creating, and that which he creates is sculpted each time beside him in the inner archivolt.

The artist has represented God in the form of Christ, thereby applying the text of the gospel of Saint John : all things were made by Him, the only begotten son.

Beginning with the lowest scene on the left, we have :

1. The Creation of Heaven and Earth.

2. The creation of day and night. It is thought that the figure on the left is probably not that of the Creator, for he has no nimbus. It is perhaps the author of Genesis, with his book on his knee, pondering on how to present the marvels of the Creation.

3. Creation of the firmament. Two angels separate the waters above from the waters belows.

God blessing his creation
(13th Century)

4. Creation of the plants.

5. Creation of the sun and moon.

6. Creation of the birds and fish. On the left, Adam in God's mind.

7. Creation of the beasts.

8. The garden of Eden.

9. At the summit of the outer archivolt is the creation of Adam of which we have

Adam in God's mind (13th Century)

already spoken. In the inner row, the beasts are brought unto Adam to be called by him.

Descending the right side of the arch, we have :

1. The creation of Eve in the outer archivolt. The scene beside it probably shows the fowls and fishes also called by man.

2. The four rivers of Eden, in both archivolts.

3. 4. Adam and Eve happy in Eden.

5. The Temptation. In the inner archivolt, Eve is tempted by the devil whispering in her ear. In the outer archivolts Adam seems to stretch out his hand to receive the apple. These statues are mutilated.

6. Adam and Eve hide under a tree.

7. They appear before God, now a stern judge.

8. They are driven from Eden. In the outer order, an angel wields the flaming sword.

9. Adam delving and Eve spinning. In the outer archivolt God blesses their work.

At the top of the gable, the seated figure of God blesses this world where sin and grace co-exist. — On each side an angel holds a taper. Beneath them two others swing censers.

The pillars of the bay are decorated with tall statues which it is very difficult to identify. At one time they were supposed to be the donors of the porch. Some scholars see in them more Old Testament figures.

The pedestals are carved with Old Testament scenes.

To the right, we see the story of Samuel.

1. Samuel is brought by his parents before Eli. The four figures have the names written underneath.

2. He serves God.

3. God appears to him in his sleep.

God creating Adam (13th Century)

4. The ark is taken ; Hophni and Phinehas are slain.

5. The ark, brought into the house of Dagon, causes the fall of the idol.

6. The ark is sent back on a cart drawn by two bulls.

On the pedestals to the left is the life of David. We see him :

1. As a shepherd ;

2. playing on the harp before Saul ;

3. arming himself before Saul ;

4. conquering Goliath.

II. - Right Bay

This bay is consecrated to Old Testament prefigurations of Christ, and his bride, the church.

The statues on the left are :

1. Balaam standing on his ass.

2. The queen of Sheba, a figure for the Church, leans towards Soloman. Beneath her feet is her Ethiopian slave.

3. Solomon prefiguring Christ in his wisdom, his judgement, and in having built the temple.

On the right, starting from the door :

1. Jesus, son of Sirach, the author of Ecclesiasticus. The name was formely on the scroll he carries. Under his feet, the temple whose reconstruction was wrongly attributed to him.

2. Judith is another figure for the Church in having saved her people. Her story is depicted over her head in the archivolt. Beneath her feet is a dog, the symbol of her fidelity.

3. Joseph, who was betrayed by his brothers like Jesus, Beneath him Potiphar's wife listens to the counsel of the devil.

On the lintel, the judgment of Solomon. The figures to the right represent admiring Jews.

In the tympanum is Job, whose patient suffering prefigures the passion of Jesus Christ. The composition of this scene is magnificent. Job, amongst the ashes, scrapes himself with a potsherd, whilst a grinning demon tortures him. His wife and friends are near to exhort, pity or mock him. Above, God watches the scene as if to comfort his faithful servant.

In the first archivolt, twelve angels carry the sun, the moon, the stars.

The second archivolt depicts the lives of Samson, to the left, and Gideon, to the right.

Left side :

1. A lion.

2. Samson's parents offer a sacrifice.

3. He kills the lion.

4. He finds honey in the lion's mouth.

5. He carries off the gates of Gaza.

Right side :

1. A dragon.

2. Gideon is visited by an angel while winnowing his corn.

3. He offers a sacrifice.

4. He wrings the dew out of the fleece, " a bowl full of water ".

5. Dressed in mediaeval armour, he leads two Madianites to captivity.

The third archivolt gives the stories of Esther and Judith, both women being figures of the Virgin, who also saved her people.

Left side :

1. Ahasuerus.

2. He weds Esther.

3. He is seen with Haman and Mordecai.

4. Mordecai speaks with Esther's eunuch and gives him a copy of the decree that was to destroy the Jews.

5. Esther kneels at the king's feet.

6. Mordecai sends a messenger with copies of the letters favourable to the Jews.

Right Side :

1. The head of Holofernes.

2. Judith converses with king Ozias and reproaches him for consenting to surrender the town.

3. She covers her head with ashes and prays in her oratory.

4. She leaves the town with her servant.

5. She kneels at the feet of Holofernes. Esther, opposite, is seen in the same attitude.

6. She has cut off the head, which her servant is thrusting into a sack.

In the fourth archivolt is the story of Tobias, who, according to

M. Mâle prefigures Christ in that he restored his father's sight as did Christ unto his people. Starting with the lowest scene on the left, and working round the arch, we have :

1. A crowned head.

2. Tobias and his son preparing a feast. He is told of the death of a Jew.

3. Tobias burying a Jew.

4. Tobias becomes blind.

5. Tobias conversing with his wife.

6. Tobias sends his son with letters to Gabelus.

7. Tobias blesses his son, who is about to set out. An angel is present.

8. Tobias on his journey, with his dog. An angel.

9. Tobias, guided by the angel, catches fish.

10. The meeting of Tobias and Raguel, Sarah's father.

11. Tobias and Sarah, his wife, praying in the nuptial chamber.

12. Raphaël binding the demon Asmodeus.

13. Tobias, curing his father.

14. A crowned head.

The decoration of the outer arch seems to continue the idea of God's reconciliation with man through work, and to answer that of the left bay containing a promise.

In the first archivolt are the twelve labours of the months ; in the second, the corresponding signs of the Zodiac, to which are added, near January on the left, a figure of " Hiemps " (Winter) ; on the right, near December, a naked figure of Summer. — It should be noted that Cancer is here a Crayfish : Sagittarius, as on the west door, is a Centaur.

The labours ascribed to the various months differ somewhat from those represented on the west door. Beginning on the left and working round the arch, we see :

1. January, a two-headed Janus holding a cake and a cup of wine.

2. February, a hooded figure, warms himself by a fire.

3. March prunes his vine.

4. April holds a handful of corn.

5. May, with a falcon on his fist.

6. June, a mower going to the fields, his scythe on his shoulder and a whetstone in his hand.

7. July, a man with a bundle of flax on his shoulder ; he may be going to steep flax, his robe being raised and his shoes off, as if he were to step into water.

8. August, a harvester.

9. September, a vintager treading the grapes.

10. October, a sower.

11. November, a man knocking down acorns for his pigs.

12. December, killing his pig.

In the outer archivolt, on the left, is first Winter represented by a serf, shivering and covered with snow. He has taken off his boots to warm his feet.

Then follow the signs of the Zodiac : 1. Capricorn - 2. Aquarius - 3. Pisces - 4. Aries - 5. Taurus - 6. Gemini - 7. Cancer - 8. Leo - 9. Virgo - 10. Libra - 11. Scorpio - 12. Sagittarius. At the bottom is Summer.

In the gable, as in the left bay, a bishop blesses between two angels.

The outer statues, with the exception of two, no doubt represent Old Testament figures, though impossible to identify.

On the pedestals are the Arts.

On the left :

Agriculture represented by Adam watching Abel who keeps his flocks, and Caïn who digs.

Music represented by Jubal playing on his lyre.

Metallurgy : Tubal-Caïn striking on an anvil.

Medecine, perhaps Hippocrates.

On the right :

Geometry or Architecture, carrying ruler and compasses.

Painting, with a rectangular palette.

Philosophy.

Magic, a sorcerer with a winged dragon at his feet.

The two statues which do not belong to the Old Testament are those of the right pillar, which look westward.

They represent : Saint Potentian, the archbishop of Sens who was supposed to have brought Christianity to Gaul ; and Saint Modesta, the daughter of the Roman governor Quirinus, one of the first martyrs of Chartres. On the pedestals are scenes of their martyrdoms.

III. - Left Bay

The jamb, lintel and tympanum figures depict the Incarnation and the small figures in the archivolts above open up a vista on the state of perfection which man can reach, being reconciled with God.

Saint Modesta
(13th Century)

Two groups, on the sides of the door : the Annunciation to the left, the Visitation to the right, are preceded by two figures of the prophets of the Incarnation, standing on dragons. These prophets are : Isaiah on the left (his head is broken) facing Daniel on the right. The statue of Gabriel, stands on a devil ; and Mary, by his side, is treading a serpent underfoot. On the right, the Virgin has the burning bush beneath her feet, a symbol for the Immaculate Conception.

The lintel and tympanum show the Virgin in the mysteries of her joys. On the left of the lintel, we see another Nativity, while, on the right, the Angel appears to the shepherds. In the tympanum, there is an Adoration of the Magi to the left ; and, to the right, they are warned in their sleep not to go back to Herod.

The first archivolt of the arch has ten angels, the two lowest standing on dragons, the others on clouds.

In the second archivolt we see, on the left, four Foolish Virgins, bare-headed, their lamps upside down ; on the right, four wise Virgins with veiled heads and lamps burning. The other two are placed at the bottom of the third archivolt.

The rest of the third archivolt represents the triumph of the Virtues over the Vices, which are trodden under foot. On the left are the four Cardinal Virtues starting from the bottom : 1. Prudence with an open book at her feet. Folly is a woman eating a pebble ; 2. Justice with scales, which Injustice tries to falsify ; 3. Strength in a coat of mail, holds a sword and a lion ; 4. Temperance with a dove, and intemperence uncovering her breast. On the right are the three theological Virtues : 1. Faith, with a chalice in which she receives the blood of the Lamb ; at her feet, Infidelity with eyes bandaged ; 2. Hope looks to Heaven, and Despair stabs herself ; 3. Charity clothing a beggar, and Avarice hoarding her gold. To balance the four Virtues on the opposite side, Humility with a dove ; at her feet, Pride is falling headlong.

The fourth archivolt has twelve queens holding scrolls which formerly bore their names. They symbolise the fruits of the spirit, twelve in number according to the Vulgate (Gal. V, 22-23).

The contemplative life :
she opens her book
(13th Century)

In the first archivolt of the outer arch the row of figures to the left shows the virtuous woman in Proverbs, who " seeketh wool and flax, and worketh willingly with her hands" in six of her occupations. 1. She washes wool ; 2. she cards it ; 3. she strips flax ; 4. she cards it ; 5. she spins ; 6. she winds.

Opposite are six figures of the woman who has chosen the Contemplative Life. 1. She prays before opening her book ; 2. she opens it ; 3. she reads ; 4. she meditates ; 5. she teaches ; 6. she is rapt into a trance, ecstasy being the consummation and reward of the Contemplative Life.

In the second archivolt, a row of fourteen small figures represent the Beatitudes of the body and the soul. They are represented as queens, haloed, with shields and pennants.

Starting with the lowest figure on the left, and working round the arch, we have :

1. Beauty, with four roses on her shield.
2. Liberty, with two crowns.
3. Honour, with two mitres.
4. Joy, with an angel.
5. Pleasure, also with an angel.
6. Swiftness, with three arrows.
7. Strength, with a lion.
8. Concord, with two pairs of doves.
9. Friendship, with the same.
10. Longevity, with an angel.
11. Power, with three sceptres.
12. Health, with three fish.
13. Security, with a castle.
14. Wisdom, with a dragon.

In the gable, a bishop blesses between two angels.

The statues decorating the pillars of the bay were destroyed during the French Revolution. The two outer ones, under the Beatitudes, were the Synagogue and the Church ; the two inner ones, under Active and Contemplative Life, Martha and Mary.

On the pedestals of the four statues, the conflict of the Virtues and Vices, is again represented. On the right pillar, we still see " Fortitudo " tranpling on " Crudelitas " in the shape of a lion ; and " Justinia " piercing the ape " Curiositas ".

Christ as a teacher (13th Century)

THE SOUTH PORCH

THIRTEENTH CENTURY

The outer porch, built with the inner doorways, measures 31.24 meters in length and 7.30 meters in depth. It is approached by a flight of 17 steps, and comprises three bays with pointed arches, each surmounted by a gable decorated with a niche and a cross, and supported on square pillars.

The whole of the south porch is consecrated to a glorification of Jesus Christ. He is here with His church. His apostles stand on either side of Him ; on His right are martyrs, and on His left, confessors.

I. - Central Bay

On the trumeau is a statue of Christ, the teacher of mankind, a book in his left hand, his right uplifted in blessing, and, behind his head, the cruciform nimbus. His feet rest on a lion and a dragon, the two animals usually selected from the four mentioned in the ninety-first Psalm : *Super aspidem et basiliscum ambulabis et conculcabis leonem et draconem.* At Amiens, the asp and the basilisk are placed under the two other animals. Christ's head is as fine as, if not finer than that of the famous " Beau Dieu " of Amiens. Here he is not the Christ of the Revelation, as on the western door, but the preceptor, the shepherd who gave his life for our ransom, whose love may be considered his highest quality.

For this reason, two scenes, under Christ, symbolize acts of charity. The first shows a man on his knees, who, before giving loaves to be distributed among the poor, seems to offer them to

Apostles (13th Century)

Apostles (13th Century)

Our Lord, thus calling down the heavenly blessing on his alms. — Below, a man and a woman are giving a loaf to a beggar. They are generally supposed to represent the donors of the porch : Pierre Mauclerc, Count of Dreux, and his wife, Alix of Brittany.

On each side of the door, on beautiful twisted columns, are ranged the twelve Apostles, each with a halo behind his head and barefooted. Whereas some are easy to recognize on account of their attributes, others, as in the Romanesque period (except Peter with the keys), have no special symbol, even though they carry the instruments of their deaths, several of these are identical.

Saint Peter, as head of the Church, is placed on the right hand of Christ, and is recognized at once by his curly hair and beard, and his keys, the symbols of his powers of " binding and loosing on earth ". On the carved socle, is Simon the Magician, with a huge purse hanging from his neck.

Saint Andrew carries his cross, the draperies of his cloak falling in the most graceful way.

On the left of Christ :

Saint Paul, bald, carries a sheathed sword, and there is no doubt that in fact he was beheaded.

Saint John, a beardless youth, in the garb of a priest, holds a book in his left hand, and, in the other, what is left of a palm, a symbol of his chastity. Under his feet, a man seems to offer him a cup full of serpents (an allusion to one of his miracles).

The third apostle, Saint James the Major, wears a belt of shells across his right shoulder.

The fourth is Saint James the Minor.

The fifth is Saint Bartholomew, who, until recently, held the knife with which he was flayed alive.

These are the apostles whose identify can be ascertained.

Beneath most of them are the crowned figures of Roman Emperors who persecuted them.

Tympanum, lintel and arch.

Above the door, the Last Judgment is depicted according to the gospel of Saint Mattew and the commentaries of medieval doctors.

The Last Judgement
(13th Century)

In the tympanum, Mary on one side and, on the other, Saint John, the beloved disciple, pleads for mankind, while Christ, as a judge seated on a bench, calls attention to his five wounds with a gesture of his raised hands, exposing to view his side and feet. Six angels, who carry the instruments of the Passion, remind every Christian, as plainly as do the wounds, that the power to judge was given Christ on account of his sacrifice. The angel near Saint John has the pillar and the scourge ; the one behind the Virgin, the lance. Above, four others, carry the crown of thorns, the nails and the cross.

In the archivolts, the nine choirs of Angels represent the heavenly Court of Christ. They are assigned their places according to the " Celestial Hierarchy ", which is a book wrongly attributed to Saint Dionysius the Areopagite. First come the Seraphim, to the left, and the Cherubin, to the right, who are very much alike, with six wings to symbolise the swiftness of their thought. The Seraphim personify fire and what they hold appear to be spheres, intended no doubt to represent the " live coal " with which one of them touched the lips of Isaiah. The Cherubim carry flames, for they personify light.

The following archivolts contain : the Thrones, which are indicated by seated figures with sceptres and crowns ; the Dominations, also sitting, sword in hand ; the Powers and Principalities ; finally the Archangels and Angels, the messengers of God unto men, the former fighting the demon, the latter bearing torches and censers.

Four angels blow their trumpets to announce the ressurection.

At the blast (second row of the arch), the dead arise still wrapped in their shrouds, lifting their tombstones. Their attitude is one of imploring, while a few hardened sinners, pressing one hand on their bosom, assume the spirit of protest.

In the middle of the lintel, Saint Michael is weighing souls (the beam of his scales is broken). To the left, in the lower scale, is a tiny soul shown as a naked child ; to the right, in the upper scale, a demon and two loathsome toads represent the weight of deadly sins : and another devil, so as to deceive the archangel on the merits of the blessed soul and win it to hell, tries to pull this scale down.

On Michael's left the Damned are led to eternal fire by demons, while angels on high drive them from God's presence with swords and shields. In the procession are seen a layman, a monk, a lady, a bishop, a king, all urged on toward the furnace into which one demon is hurling a woman he carries on his back. Through the flames, faces are seen to emerge out of the jaws of Leviathan.

The scene is continued across the archivolts to the right. First comes a devil who carries a woman on his shoulder ; next to this, another attends a princess ; a third holds a nun ; a fourth torments a miser, with his purse hanging from his neck ; and a fifth drags along a naked woman whose long hair sweeps the ground.

On the other side of the lintel, the righteous make up the procession of the Blessed. They are welcomed by an angel who leads them, while others, from heaven, honour them with censers. In this new procession, again we find a king, a bishop, a monk, a virgin, and laymen, one of whom wears a wreath of flowers.

The lowest row of the arch represents Paradise. On his covered hands, an angel is bringing a soul to Abraham's bosom where three are already enfolded. Then an angel conducts a man wearing a crown ; another guides a virgin, and a third welcomes a King who, in a spirit of humility, has offered to God his crown, held by an angel. The blessed are naked as a sign of their purity.

On the brackets supporting the lintel, two little figures are carved. The one on the side of Hell weeps, and is an emblem of sorrow.

The one on the side of Heaven laughs as an emblem of joy.

Such is this Last Judgment, which was perhaps the favourite subject of the thirteenth century artist.

The decoration of the porch proper represents the Heavenly Court.

The inner archivolt of the outer arch has twenty-eight statuettes of kings and queens of the Old Testament : we recognize David with his harp, Solomon with a sceptre, and the queen of Sheba holding a flower in her left hand. At the top, the four major prophets, bearded, talk with four minor prophets who are clean-shaven.

The second archivolt is carved with fourteen figures of exquisite workmanship. They are the fourteen Beatitudes described by Saint Anselme and Saint Bernard, representing the seven gifts of the body and the seven gifts of the soul which are promised to the faithful in the life to come. These beatitudes are, for the body : beauty, swifness, strength, liberty, health, pleasure, longevity ; for the soul : wisdom, friendship, concord, honour, power, security, joy.

The heavenly court is completed on the inner faces of the outer pillars where the twenty-four elders of the Apocalypse are sculpted, seated and crowned, holding musical instruments and vials of perfume.

The outer faces of these piers show the Virtues and Vices which are called to account on the day of Judgment. Each of the twelve Vices, exemplified in a little anecdotic scene, is represented under the corresponding Virtue, which is a seated figure of a woman with a shield and heraldic symbol.

On the left pillar, west side, we have the three theological Virtues and their corresponding sins, i.e, starting from the top :

Faith with a chalice on her shield.

Idolatry worshipping an idol.

Pride
(13th Century)

Hope with a standard on her shield, looking up to heaven.

Despair killing herself.

Charity with a lamb on her shield, giving a cloak to a beggar.

Avarice hoarding her gold.

On the South side of the same pillar are, following the same order :

Chastity with a phœnix on her shield, holding a palm.

Lust, a man with a courtesan.

Prudence with a serpent.

Folly, a half-naked, dishevelled person carrying a club.

Humility with a dove.

Pride falling from his horse.

On the right pillar, south side, we see :

Docility with an ox on her shield, a mutilated figure.

Indocility, a woman who holds a drawn sword between herself and a monk.

Gentleness with a lamb.

Harshness, a noble lady thrusting out her foot against a servant who kneels before her.

Strength in a coat of mail over her robes, with a helmet on her head, a sword in her right hand and a lion on her shield.

Saint Maurice
(13th Century)

Cowardice running from a hare.

East side :

Perseverance with a crown on her shield.

Inconstancy, a monk who has doffed his gown and leaves the monastery.

Obedience with a camel.

Disobedience, a man striking his bishop.

Concord, holding an olive-twig on her shield.

Discord, a quarrel between husband and wife : a distaff is thrown into a corner, the jug is upset.

In the gable, the Holy Virgin, a pattern of Christian perfection.

II. - Left Bay of the Martyrs

The eight tall statues placed against the columns on the right and left of the door, are those of martyrs. The two outer ones are among the finest of the cathedral and belong to the period when the porch was added. They represent, on the left, Saint Maurice " the very image of the perfect knight " ; on the right, Saint George. Both wear the military dress and armour of the thirteenth century. — Working towards the door, on the left, is Saint Stephen in deacon's dress ; Saint Clement pope ; Saint Lawrence as a deacon again. On the right, we have Saint Piat in the dress of a priest ; Saint Denis, bishop of Paris ; Saint Vincent as a deacon.

Under each one of these eight statues is a scene reminding us of some detail of their martyrdom. Thus, under Saint George, is the wheel on to which he died.

The story of the martyrdom of Saint Stephen is shown in the bottom of the archivolts and in the lintel. At the base of the left archivolts he is talking with Jews : in the left part of the lintel he is lead to his death : on the right he is stoned. At the base of the right archivolts Saul, the future Paul, prevents the saint's clothes from being taken by his murderers.

In the tympanum, Christ, the victim or martyr par excellence, stands crowned between two kneeling angels.

In the first archivolt, eight children sit holding palms and spheres (which stand for the seal of God) : they are the Holy Innocents.

The second illustrates the verse of the Book of Revelation concerning those who have washed their robes in the blood of the Lamb. We see six seated figures holding out their mantles to receive the blood that flows in two streams, issuing from the throat of a ram whose head is in the keystone.

In the third, eight martyrs hold palms.

In the fourth are ten kings and bishops.

The fifth gives a hierarchy of the martyrs in twelve statues of levites, deacons, priests, abbots, bishops ; at the top, an Emperor and a Pope, who were two equal powers in the middle ages.

The outer arch again is adorned with carvings. Firstly are represented, on the left, the five Wise Virgins with their lamps trimmed and filled ; on the right, the five Foolish Virgins.

The second archivolt consists of ten figures of Angels. The lowest on the left stands on a wheel and therefore is a Throne. The lowest on the right is an Archangel trampling on a dragon. All the others merely hold tapers.

In the gable, Saint Anne holds a vase with a lily.

The decoration of the left pillar helping to support the vaulting, consists of twenty-four bas reliefs of martyrdoms which it would be presumptuous to identify with certainty.

On the south face of the pillar, starting from the top, we have :

1. Saint John the Baptist being beheaded.

2. Saint Denis holding his scalp.

3. Saint Saturninus dragged down the steps of the Capital of Toulouse by a bull.

4. A martyr, beheaded.

5. Saint Procope thrown into a furnace.

6. A martyr tied to a tree.

West side :

1. A martyr cast into a well or an oven.

2. Saint Cyprien on the point of being beheaded.

3. Saint Ignatius between two lions.

4. Saint Theodore torn with a rake.

5. Saint Eustace with his wife and children burn in the brazen bull.

6. Saint Gervais scourged to death and Saint Protais pierced with a lance.

North side :

1. Saint Clement thrown into the sea.

2. A martyr kneeling.

3. Saint Lambert on the point of being beheaded.

4. Saint Vitus and Saint Modestus in a boiling cauldron.

5. A martyr being scourged.

6. Saint Quentin at the stake.

East face :

1. Saint Thomas of Canterbury put to death at the altar.

2. Saint Blasius being flayed alive.

3. Saint Leger having his eyes put out.

4. Saint Vincent washed ashore in spite of the millstone round his neck ; a crow protects the corpse from a wolf.

5. Saint Lawrence on the gridiron.

6. Saint Cheron, with his head in his hands, stands near a well.

The pillar on the right does not belong to this bay as far as the decoration is concerned, and the scenes carved on it have been described in relation with the central bay.

III. - Right Bay of the Confessors

The right doorway is decorated with statues of Confessors of the Christian faith. The two outside figures, added when the porch was built, are local saints : Saint Laumer, a monk of Perche, to the left ; and to the right, Saint Avitus, abbot of Micy. Reading towards the door, first from the left, are Saint Silvester, pope ; Saint Ambrose, archbishop of Milan ; Saint Nicholas, bishop of Myra. On the right, in the same order, are Saint Gregory, pope ; Saint Jerome holding a Bible ; Saint Martin, bishop of Tours.

The subjects carved beneath them are extremely varied. Thus, under Saint Jerome, a woman with her eyes bandaged represents the Synagogue. Elsewhere we see allusions to miracles worked by the saints ; for instance two dogs lick Saint Martin's crosier because he is said to have stopped them from pursuing a hare.

The lintel and tympanum illustrate the stories of Saint Martin and Saint Nicholas, the two saints being then extremely popular.

On the left, Saint Martin on horseback meets a beggar at the gate of Amiens, and gives him half of his cloak. Above this scene, we see him asleep, his servant lying a little lower, and Christ appears to him clad in that portion of the cloak that was given to the beggar (the other half hangs on the wall).

The scene on the right of the lintel represents Saint Nicholas dropping a purse into the house of a poor sick man about to sell his three daughters into prostitution. The purse contains their dowries. The top scene shows sick people who have come to be cured by the miraculous oils oozing from the saint's tomb. A few have brought vessels as if to take away some of the precious ointment.

On either side of the lintel, the lowest row of the arch tells the story of Saint Giles. On the left, he is seen with his doe. On the right is an episode of Charlemagne's life.

When the great Emperor went to Spain, he stopped to visit Saint Giles. In the carving, we see Saint Giles celebrating mass, while an angel appears with a scroll on which is written a sin Charles had tried to keep secret. The scene, which seems to have been a favourite one, is also related in the windows.

The remaining part of the arch is filled with a hierarchy of the Confessors. They all have halos behind their heads and carry the special attributes of their ranks or dignities.

We see laymen, knights, monks, priests, abbots, kings, bishops, archbishops ; at the top of the fifth order, as equal in rank, a Pope and an Emperor.

The first order of the outer arch is carved with ten figures of apostles.

The second order has a row of ten angels, most of whom hold censers ; the lowest on the left is an Archangel standing on a lion ; the lowest on the right is a Throne.

Saint Martin
(13th Century)

In the gable, the Virgin, between two angels, holds the book of faith open against her.

The left pillar of this bay has already been described in relation with the central bay. On the right pillar are carved in low-relief twenty-four anecdotic scenes of the lives of the confessors.

South side, starting from the top :

1. Saint Gregory the Great writes, prompted by a dove which is perched on his shoulder, while his young secretary draws back a curtain to peer into this mystery.

2. Saint Remy anointing Clovis.

3. Clovis kneels before a bishop (Saint Solennis) (?).

4. Saint Laumer (?) curing a sick person.

5. Saint Calais.

6. Saint Paul Hermit, conversing with Saint Anthony (?).

West side :

1. Saint Leo praying on the tomb of Saint Peter.

2. Saint Martin blessing a man who wanted to kill him.

Saint Thomas A Becket of Canterbury (13th Century)

3. Saint Lubin anointing Saint Caletric (?).

4. An abbot resting.

5. Saint Anthony tempted by the devil while he is reading the Scriptures.

6. A meditating Saint.

North side :

1. Saint Ambrose is preaching to Saint Augustine.

2. A Saint working a miracle.

3. A bishop leading a dragon with his stole.

4. Saint Giles curing one possessed.

5. Saint Jerome translating the Bible.

6. A Saint driving back temptation.

East side :

1. Saint Sylvester baptizing Emperor Constantine.

2. A Saint Brings a child to life again.

3. Saint Caletric visiting Saint Lubin (?).

4. Saint Benedict blesses a poisoned cup.

5. A confessor converses with a kneeling peasant.

6. A saint confronting a winged dragon.

Finally, between the gables, the south porch is surmounted by pinnacles in the arcades of which are placed eighteen kings. The first one only, on the west side, can be identified as David playing his harp : at his feet, a tree of Jesse sprouts from the breast of a man reclining. The whole row thus proves to represent the lineage of Christ, and link the Old Testament to the New.

The choir screen (16th Century)

THE SCREEN

SIXTEENTH TO EIGHTEENTH CENTURY

No sooner had Jean Texier or Jean de Beauce completed the northern spire than the canons asked him to build a screen round the chancel, as they no longer wished to leave it open to the public. The two first arches on the right and left were immediately walled in, the work being carried on as far as the main altar, which then stood at the end of the second bay of the choir. It is in the flamboyant style of the period. When, a little later,

The Screen (18th Century)

in 1520, the altar was moved backward, the work was resumed, and completed in 1530 in the flamboyant and Renaissance styles.

As for the forty niches destined to contain statues telling the lives of the Virgin and of Christ, twenty-four were yet to be filled. This was done gradually depending on the funds available, and the last groups were not placed until 1714.

The first four groups on the south side are the work of Jean Soulas, a Parisian sculptor (1520-1525).

1. Joachim is visited by an angel, who announces the forthcoming birth of the Virgin.

2. At home, Saint Anne receives the same visitation.

3. Anne and Joachim embrace in front of the Golden Gate of Jerusalem.

4. The Birth of the Virgin.

The three following groups, commissioned in 1520, are also the work of Jean Soulas.

5. Mary is brought to the temple, and is seen ascending the steps by herself.

6. She marries Joseph before the high priest, Saint Anne and two other witnesses.

7. The Annunciation. Mary, to the right, kneeling under a canopy, turns round towards the Angel. Between them is set the symbolic lily.

The five following groups, added a little later, are probably the work of the same artist.

8. The visitation.

Between this group and the next, we see the dial of one of those complicated clocks that, not content with pointing out the time, also told the day of the week, the month of the year, the hour of sunrise and sunset, the phase of the moon and the sign of the Zodiac. The works were partially destroyed in 1793. The turret on the left contained the stairs leading up to the clock.

9. Joseph's dream on the left ; on the right, Mary is sewing.

10. The Nativity. Mary, Joseph, and a group of angels are worshipping the new-born babe. The shepherds, together with the ox and the ass, are sculpted to the right.

11. The Circumcision.

12. The Adoration of the Magi, one of whom is a negro. They are dressed as French courtiers of the time.

The next two groups are the work of François Marchand, from Orléans (1542).

13. The Presentation at the temple. Simeon is the only figure. left of the original group.

14. The massacre of the Innocents.

The sewing Virgin
(16th Century)

15. The Baptism of Christ is by Nicholas Guybert (1543).

The next three groups are by Thomas Boudin (1612).

16. The Temptation of Christ in the wilderness, on the temple, and on the mountain,

17. The woman of Canaan whom the disciples try to send away.

18. The transfiguration.

19. The woman taken in adultery, the work of Jean de Dieu from Arles (1681). — Jesus is writing on the ground.

20. Jesus restores sight to the man who was born blind. The group is by Legros (1682).

Between this group and the next, and just at the curve of the apse is a space with no canopy. Before the Revolution, the relics of Saint Piat, Saint Lubin, and others used to be exposed there. Now we see Saint Martin giving half of his cloak to a beggar.

21, 22. The Triumphal Entry into Jerusalem by Jean Tuby (1703).

The seven following groups are the work of Simon Mazières (1714).

23. Gethsemane.

24. The Betrayal.

25. The Trial of Jesus.

26. The Scourging.

27. Jesus crowned with thorns.

28. The Crucifixion.

29. The Deposition.

The next four groups are the work of the same Thomas Boudin we saw on the south side. Their date is 1611.

30. The Resurrection.

31. The Women at the Sepulchre.

32. The journey to Emmaus.

33. The apparition of Jesus to Thomas.

The remaining groups, are the work of an unknown artist and were carved about 1520.

34. Christ appears to the Virgin.

The Virgin in the adoration of the Magi (16th Century)

35. The Ascension.

36. The Pentecost.

37. The Virgin and Saint John adore the Cross.

38. The Virgin's death.

39. Her Assumption. The body is raised by four angels, Christ witnessing the scene.

41. Her Coronation. The three persons of the Trinity are placing the crown on her head.

Set in the screen are small rooms used as chapels, and in the past by night-watchmen.

The second carved door on the south side, where the open work has been quite recently restored, leads to the room, formerly a chapel, where the bellringer used to sleep.

The famous blue Virgin
(12th Century)
Cl. Laniepce

The nativity (12th Century)

THE WINDOWS

Every window is given a number according to the plan at the end of this book. There are, therefore, one-hundred and sixty seven windows in the cathedral, roses, oculi, and lancets.

Almost all the windows are read from left to right beginning at the base. A diagram will be given for each window that is an exception to this rule.

Unless special mention is made to the contrary the glass at Chartres is early thirteenth century work.

We begin this description with the three lancets which are placed under the West rose — unrivalled in their beauty, and perhaps the best example of twelfth century workmanship. Together with the Blue Virgin, they belonged to the former cathedral severely damaged in the fire of 1194.

1. - THE JESSE WINDOW

This window to the right represents the genealogy of Christ in the shape of a family tree. — In the first medallion, Jesse is seen asleep, and a tree sprouts from his loins. The six panels of the stem contain in succession four kings, the Virgin, then Christ with the seven doves, the symbols of the seven Gifts of the Holy Spirit. To right and left, prophets who announced the coming of Christ.

2. - THE LIFE OF OUR LORD

(1, 2, 3) Annunciation Visitation, Nativity. (4) The apparition of the angels to the shepherds. (5, 6) The meeting of Herod and the Magi. (7, 8) The adoration of the Magi. (9) Their journey back. (10, 11) The Presentation at the temple. (12) The dream of the Magi. (13, 14, 15) The Massacre of the Innocents. (16, 17, 18) Flight to and return from Egypt. (19) The fall of the Egyptian idols. (20) The Baptism of Christ. (21) A dream of Joseph. (22, 23, 24) The Entry into Jerusalem.

3. - THE PASSION WINDOW

(1) Transfiguration. (2) Christ comes down Mount Tabor with the three disciples. (3) The Last Supper. (4) Jesus washes the apostles'feet. (5) The Betrayal. (6) The scourging of Jesus. (7, 8) Crucifixion and Deposition. (9) The Annointing. (10) The Holy Women at the Sepulchre. (11) Mary Magdalene tells the disciples of the Resurrection. (12) The apparition of Christ to the Holy Women. (13, 14) The meeting then the supper with the disciples of Emmaus.

A description will now be given of the sixty-four lower storey lancets and oculi, starting next to the south tower.

4. - THE STORY OF S. JOHN THE DIVINE

(1) A flight to Egypt. (2, 3) The armourers as donors of the window. (4) Death of Stactacus. (5) S. John is banished to Patmos. (6) He writes the Book of Revelation. (7) He is summoned before Aristomedes. (8) On entering Ephesus, S. John brings a woman back to life. (9) Eye-witnesses marvel at the miracle. (10) S. John drinks out of the poisoned cup. (11) Two young men breaking up gems. (12) S. John making the gems whole again. (13) Christ appears to S. John. (14) S. John changing wood into gold and pebbles into gems. (15) A young man hands his treasure to a money-changer. (16) S. John awaiting his death. (17, 18, 19) Angels.

5. - THE STORY OF MARY MAGDALENE

(1, 2, 3) The water-carriers, donors of the window. (4) Mary Magdalene at Simon's house. (5) Death of Lazarus. (6, 7) His funeral. (8) Martha and Mary and Jesus on their way to the grave. (9) Jesus comes to the grave. (10) The raising of Lazarus from the dead. (11) Mary Magdalene at the Sepulchre. (12) The apparition of Jesus in the garden. (13, 14) Mary Magdalene telling the disciples of the Resurrection. (15) Mary Magdalene lands in Provence. (16, 17) Her brother St. Maximin preaches. (18) The death of Mary Magdalene. (19) Her entombment. (20, 21) Jesus receives her soul. (22) An angel holding a censer.

6. - THE PARABLE OF THE GOOD SAMARITAN

See the diagram, page 84.

This window, whilst telling the parable of the Good Samaritan, illustrates a commentary written by the Venerable Bede, whose works were known in the medieval Ecoles de Chartres. For him, as for other earlier church fathers, the Good Samaritan is a symbol for Christ himself, and the man left on the wayside, is humanity, the victim of sin, but happily saved by the sacrifice of Christ.

(1, 2, 3) The Shoemakers, donors of the window. (4) Jesus telling the parable. (5) The man leaves Jerusalem. (6, 7) Thieves attack from behind a tree and strip him of his goods. (8) The priest and the Levite pass by. (9) The Samaritan binds his wounds. (10, 11) and brings him to an inn ; (12) takes care of him.

(13) God creating man. (14) Adam in the garden of Eden. (15) God makes a woman out of Adam's rib. (16) God forbids Adam and Eve to eat of the tree of the knowledge of good and evil. (17) They sit under the tree. (18) They are tempted by the serpent and eat the fruit of the forbidden tree. (19) God calling to them. (20) They are driven out of Eden. (21) Adam delves and Eve Spins. (22) God utters the sentence with the promise of redemption. (23) Caïn slaying Abel. (24) Jesus, the Saviour of men, of whom the Good Samaritan is but a symbol.

The Good Samaritan

7. - DEATH AND ASSUMPTION OF MARY

Three medallions show the shoemakers as donors of the window. — In the medallions of the centre, we see : the death of the Virgin surrounded by the twelve apostles ; Christ receiving her soul in the shape of a naked child ; her funeral ; angels with censers ; her entombment ; her Assumption ; her Coronation angels holding a second crown

*The death of the Virgin
(13th Century)*

— Right and left, we see holy women, apostles and angels.

8. - THE VENDOME CHAPEL

The window is a specimen of 15th century flamboyant, with curvilinear tracery and glass.

The chapel, built some time after 1413, was given by Louis de Bourbon, Count of Vendôme, and a member of the royal family.

In the lower storey, we see the donor and his wife (first group to the right), as well as other members of the royal family, all with their patron saints. Under them, their coats of arms.

In the upper storey, we behold a Coronation of the Virgin again with S. John the Baptist on the left and S. John the Divine, holding the poisoned cup, on the right.

In the upper part of the window, a Crucifixion and a Last Judgment.

9. - THE MIRACLES OF THE VIRGIN

The signature, in the left and right corners of the window, as in the bottom petal of the first quatrefoil, is that of the butchers. The rest of the quatrefoil shows the Virgin of Chartres between men dragging stones for the building of the south tower, and wine for the workers.

The other three quatrefoils are modern (1928), and due to the generosity of an Americain banker, Mr. Sachs. The first again shows workmen : an architect, masons, stone-cutters and carpenters. The second shows a procession with the shrine containing the *Sancta Camisia*. The top one represents the image of the Virgin of Chartres surrounded with angels, prophets, and two holy bishops of Chartres : S. Yves and S. Fubert.

The panels on either side are old work. But without their context; they are difficult to identify.

10. - GRISAILLE, STORY OF S. APOLLINARIS ANGELIC CHOIRS

I. (1-5) The grisaille we see at the bottom of the window was inserted in 1328, replacing older panels, taken out. It represents different saints in whose honour an altar had just been erected somewhere near the window.

II. (6) S. Apollinaris of Ravenna heals a child. (7, 8, 9) He preaches, baptises, heals the sick. (10) He goes to exile. (11) He heals a man possessed with a devil. (12, 13) He brings a woman back to life. (14) He is summoned before the judge. (15) He is imprisoned. (16) He breaks an idol. (17) Heathens. (18) He is scourged ; (19) buried. (20) A group of devout men witnessing the scene.

III. The nine orders of the angelic hierachy are represented in the nine following panels. — At the top, Christ between two angels.

11.

The white glass was put in — and the old disposed of — by the constitutional clergy (1791). Restored by François Lorin in 1971.

12. - THE STORY OF S. FULBERT
(given by the American architects)

In the same year (1791), the constitutional clergy also took out the old glass, and walled in the window to place an altar here. — The window was opened up again in the course of the nineteenth century ; and now stained glass may be seen here, the work of the local stained-glass maker, Mr. Lorin, and donated by the American Institute of Architects.

The subject chosen was S. Fulbert.

At the bottom we have a plan of the romanesque church he built, the Veil of the Virgin, and a few creations of modern architecture by way of signature. Then Fulbert is seen with a pope, next studying in Rheims, then called to Chartres. In the third, fourth and fifth registers, he is ordained a bishop, he teaches medecine, painting, theology, profane letters, he advises a sculptor. In the sixth register, the cathedral is being built, and Canute, King of England, sends alms. In the seventh and eighth registers, bishop Fulbert converses with S. Odilon of Cluny, then with monks, he writes the life of S. Giles, helps the sick and the poor. In the ninth register, the Virgin cures him with three drops of her milk. In the tenth, on his death-bed, he repels a heretic, and he dies in the top pane.

13. - THE STORY OF S. ANTHONY AND S. PAUL THE ANCHORITE

(1, 2) Donors : the fishmongers. (3) In church, S. Anthony hears the gospel of the day. (4) He distributes all that he has to the poor. (5) He leaves his sister in the care of nuns. (6) He speaks to a hermit. (7) He digs. (8, 9) He is tempted by the devil in the shape of a woman, then of a dwarf. (10) He talks to a man. (11, 12, 13, 14) He is beaten by demons. (15) He reads in his cell. (16) He visits S. Paul the anchorite. A raven brings them bread. (17) On his way back, he sees the soul of S. Paul lifted up by angels. (18) He prays near the kneeling corpse of S. Paul. (19) The burial of S. Paul. (20, 21) S. Anthony leaves his mantle to a disciple. He dies.

14. - THE TEMPTATION OF CHRIST. THE MARRIAGE-FEAST IN CANA. THE BLUE VIRGIN

The lowest row shows the three temptations of Christ ; (1) in the wilderness ; (2) on the pinnacle of the temple ; (3) up into an exceeding high mountain.

The marriage-feast of Cana is given in six episodes : (4) Jesus is going to the feast. (5) The feast. (6) The mother of Jesus says to him : They have no wine. (7) She says to the servants : Whatsoever he saith unto you, do it. (8) Jesus makes the water into wine. (9) A servant bears the wine to the governor of the feast.

The upper part of the window is filled with a large figure of the Virgin of Chartres, framed in with smaller figures of angels supporting her throne on columns, or worshipping her. The four panels of the Virgin herself, of blue glass on a ground of ruby, are a masterpiece of twelfth century workmanship. The face is modern, and very different from the tawny face of the Child, which is so stern and expressive.

15.

In the oculus above the two windows, the Virgin stands crowned and suckling the Child.

16. - THE STORY OF THE VIRGIN

The panels to the right and left corners show the donors : (1) the vinegrowers ; (2) Count Thibault VI of Champagne who gave the window at the request of " Thomas, Count of Perche ", killed at the battle of Lincoln (1217). The approximate date of the glass is given thereby.

Then follows the life of the Virgin according to the aprocryphal as well as the canonical gospels.

(3) Joachim and Ann spurned by the high priest. (4, 5) Joachim and Ann are visited by an angel. (6) They meet at the Golden Gate. (7) At home they await the fulfilment of the promise. (8, 9) The birth and bath of Mary. (10) Mary is brought to a teacher (provided with a birch). (11) She is at school. (12) The miracle of Joseph's flowering stem. (13) The betrothal of Mary and Joseph.

(14, 15, 16) Annunciation, Visitation, Nativity. (17) The angels bring the good tidings to the shepherds. (18) The Presentation at the temple. (19, 20, 21) Herod sending forth the Magi, one of whom is still passing through the gates of Jerusalem, while another is already paying his homage to Jesus. (22, 23, 24) Flight to Egypt. The massacre of the Innocents, presided over by Herod. (25) Jesus blessing some unknown people.

17. - THE ZODIAC WINDOW

Donors. — The two medallions (1, 3) show the same donors as those of the former window. Between them (2), a bell-ringer and two men. Lower still, at both ends of the border, we see the busts of two vine-growers carrying their hoes over their shoulders.

The signs of the Zodiac are generally represented in the round medallions to the right. The special labour of the corresponding month is figured on the left. The central quatrefoils contain both a sign and a monthly labour. (4) January with three heads (the past, the present and the coming year, together with Aquarius. (5, 6) February, a man in a hood before a fire. Pisces. (7, 8) March, a vinepruner. Aries. (9) May, a knight goes hawking. Gemini. (10, 11), April with flowers. Taurus. (12, 13) June, a mower. Cancer. (14) July with his reaping-hook. Leo. (15, 16) August threshing his corn. Virgo. (17,

The Virgin suckling the child (13th Century)

18) September : the grapes are trod in a tub. Libra. (19) October : a man, astride a cask, pours wine into it. Scorpio. (20, 21) November : a man slaughters his pig. Sagittarius. (22, 23) December : a peasant feasting. Capricorn. (25) Christ, sitting between Alpha and Omega.

18.

In the oculus, Jesus on the Cross, between the Virgin and S. John. Beneath his feet, Adam and Eve.

19, 20, 21.

These three grisailles are fourteenth century work. In the first, an Annunciation of the same period. The figures in the oculus, on the contrary, are of the thirteenth century.

22, 23.

Grisailles of the seventeenth century. The older glass was probably taken out to give more light for the groups in the screen opposite, by Thomas Boudin (1612).

24. - THE STORY OF S. MARTIN

(1, 2, 3) S. Martin gives half of his cloak to a beggar, outside the gates of Amiens. A shoemaker, as donor. S. Martin, asleep, sees Jesus wearing his cloak. (4, 5, 6) A shoemaker. The baptism of S. Martin. A shoemaker, (7, 8, 9) S. Martin brings a dead man back to life. A shoemaker. S. Hilary of Poitiers welcoming him. (10, 11, 12) S. Martin tied to a tree. Two ruffians lying in ambush. S. Martin causes a tree to fall upon heathens. (13, 14, 15) He is consecrated the bishop of Tours. (16, 17, 18) Near a tomb, he forces out the soul of a robber, who was honoured as a martyr. Lookers on. He brings a child back to life. (19, 20, 21) He heals one possessed of a devil. He preaches. (22, 23, 24) He heals a sick man. (25, 26, 27) He is seen riding to the house of Tetradius to heal one possessed of a devil. (28, 29, 30) He kisses a leper. An angel with a censer. The miracle of a vessel that falls and does not break. — The rest of the window deals with the death and burial of the saint. At the top, Christ, sitting between angels, blesses the world.

25. - S. THOMAS A BECKET OF CANTERBURY

Donors, the tanners (5, 6, 7). — Under and above them, the story of S. Thomas of Canterbury, who was well-known in the diocese. (1, 2) S. Thomas and his family seem to be banished. (3) He stands in the presence of a king. (4) On horse-back, he arrives at the gates of a town. (8) He is consecrated a bishop. (9) He is in discussion with a king. (10) He embarks for France. (11) He converses with the Pope. (12, 13, 14) Cistercian monks seem to say farewell to S. Thomas, who leaves them on horseback. An interview with the French King. (15) He converses with the Pope and a King. (16) He goes back to England. (17) Again a King and a bishop. (18) The king refuses to receive S. Thomas. (19, 20, 21) He converses with men, the same who intend to murder him. He is about to enter the cathedral, his murderers, armed, wait in ambush. (22, 23) He is killed at the altar. (24, 25) The saint is lying dead, incensed by an angel. On either side, two sick persons are crouching. This is in memory of the miracles worked at the saint's tomb in Canterbury.

26. - THE STORIES OF S. MARGARET AND S. CATHERINE

See the diagram, page 92.

Donors : (1) Marguerite de Lèves, kneeling before an image of the Virgin of Chartres. (2) Her husband and brother-in-law. — This " signature " enables the historian to give the approximate date of the window (1220-1227). Four scenes concern S. Margaret of Antioch. — (3) The saint stands holding a little cross : near her an angel and a demon in the shape of a monster. (4) She fights the demon. (5, 6) Her martyrdom. Sixteen panels are consecrated to S. Catherine of Alexandria. — (7) She tries to convince Emperor Maxence of his error. (8) She is sent to prison. (9, 10) She discusses with doctors (in the presence of the Emperor), and converts them. An angel assists her. (11, 12) The emperor pronounces the sentence ; and the new converts are burnt. (13) Their souls taken up to heaven by angels. (14) Catherine, who has again refused to abjure her faith, is standing between the executioners. (15) The Queen coming to visit her in the prison.

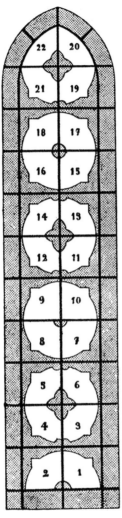

Saint Margaret and Saint Catherine

(16) Christ himself gives her Holy Communion. (17) She refuses to worship an idol. (18) The wheels on which she was to be tortured break while she is praying. (19) The Queen, who has become a Christian, suffers martyrdom. (20) She is buried. (21) Maxence, prompted by a demon, sentences Catherine to death. (22) She is beheaded.

27. - THE STORY AND MIRACLES OF S. NICHOLAS

The five lower medallions are modern. The middle one gives the date of the restoration (1923).

The story begins with the fourth medallion. — (4, 5) Birth and bath of S. Nicholas (6) The saint, refusing to suckle his mother on fast days (Wednesdays and Fridays). (7) S. Nicholas at school. (8) He throws three gold coins through a window, the dowry for the three daughters who were to be forced into prostitution by their poverty-stricken father. (9-13) He is elected, then consecrated as bishop of Myra. (14, 15) S. Nicholas going toward a harbour. A man is unloading a sack of corn to feed the people during a famine. (16-19). A Jew lends money to a Christian ; who swears, before an image of the saint, that he has given it back. In fact the coins are contained in a hollow stick that he has placed for a moment in the hand of the Jew. The baptism of the Jew, placed here for decorative purposes. A chariot kills the Christian and breaks the stick, out of which the coins gush. (20) Another Jew (wearing the pointed cap) strikes an image of the saint. (21, 22, 23) The story of the three young students killed by the innkeeper and brought back to life by the saint.

The innkeeper and his wife beg for forgiveness. (24, 25) A child falls into the sea, and is given back to his parents by the saint.

28. - THE STORY OF S. REMY

(2) An unknown donor. (1) S. Remy heals a blind man with his mother's milk. (3, 4) Some ruffians want to kill him. He is saved by a miracle, when a building collapses. (5, 6) He is elected to be the bishop of Rheims. His consecration. (7) He heals a blind-man who was possessed of a devil. (8) He converses with Queen Clothilde. (9, 10) S. Remy on his travels. (11) He preaches before King Clovis and the Queen. (12) He puts out a fire. (13, 14) S. Remy is a guest in the house of a relation, whose wine runs short. In the cellar, the wine is gushing out of the casks. (15, 16) Queen Clothilde and the bishop are in prayer. (17, 18) King Clovis is baptized, then anointed. (19) The King and the bishop converse. (20) The bishop shows the king a man surrounded with flames. (The meaning of the scene is not known). (21, 22) The bishop dies. His soul is received by an angel : note he still wears his mitre.

29.

This grisaille is thirteenth century work. It was restored in 1416, and given a St. Nicholas of that period.

30. - THE STORY OF S. SYLVESTER

This is the story of pope S. Sylvester who was a contemporary of Constantine the Great. — (1, 2, 3) The masons, as donors. (4) The saint's widowed mother brings the child to a priest. The boy already has a halo. (5) Sylvester, now a young man, welcomes a certain Timothy from Antioch. (6, 7) Timothy is beheaded. His burial. (8) Sylvester is brought before the prefect of Rome, Tarquinius, who bids him sacrifice to a golden idol, and, as the saint refuses, sends him to prison. (9) Tarquinius is choked by a fishbone. (10) Pope Melchiades takes Sylvester out of prison. (11, 12) A man kneels before Sylvester. Sylvester is ordained a priest. (13) Sylvester is chosen after the death of Melchiades. The tiara is placed on his head. (14) Emperor Constantine shows a golden idol. (15) Silvester in papal robes and tiara, shows clerks a mountainslope. (16) Constantine, stricken with leprosy, and a physician. (17) A tub, in which children will be killed, whose blood is destined to heal the Emperor, if he bathes in it. (18) The mothers lamenting at the palace-gate. (19) Constantine on his throne is issuing orders. (20) A young man speaks to women, each holding a child, no doubt telling them they have to fear no longer. (21) S. Peter and S. Paul appear to Constantine. (22) S. Sylvester receives a message from Constantine. (23) The meeting of Constantine and S. Sylvester. (24) Constantine is baptized by Pope Sylvester. (25) The pope and Emperor are visiting the site of what will become S. Peter's church in Rome. (26) They return in the Emperor's chariot. (27) A contest between S. Sylvester and a Jewish magician. (28) The magician kills a mad bull by whispering in his ear. (29) Sylvester brings the bull back to life. (30) Constantine on his throne witnesses the contest. (31) The burial of the saint. (32, 33) An angel takes his soul up to heaven. Another angel offers incense to it.

Four little round medallions on each side of this window show Emperor Constantine promulgating laws (written on scrolls) on behalf of the Church. There were seven laws. In the topmost medallion to the right, Constantine, holding a scroll on which nothing is written, looks at S. Sylvester's soul going up to heaven.

31.

A grisaille with the figure of S. Piat in ecclesiastical robes. It dates from some time after the building of the S. Piat chapel (1350-58).

32. - THE STORY OF S. PAUL

The first five rows are modern, except for two medallions. Their date is that of the restoration of the Apostles' Chapel, 1872. — The scenes are mostly taken from the Acts.

(1) Saul is seen riding out of Jerusalem. (2) A light shines above him from heaven, and he falls to earth. (3) A man stands near the gate of Damas. (This is an old panel). (5) S. Paul sailing to Italy. (6) After landing in Malta, he is warming himself near a fire, and shaking off a viper that had fastened on his hand. (7) He is healing the father of Publius, chief man of the island. — Now we seem to return to the first episode : (8) Barnabas is bringing S. Paul to S. Peter. (9) S. Paul's escape from Damascus. (10) The saint is struck by a man (an old panel). (11) He blesses a man sitting by a door. (12) A baptism (copied from panel 24). (13) Two men conversing near a door. (14) A baptism (imitated from panel 16). (15) The saint talks to men advancing toward him. (16, 17) S. Paul baptises : first, a man standing in the font ; then, a dying man. (18) He is led by an angel, seemingly towards the preceding scene. (19) An apostle, standing before a group of listeners, seems to be looking at S. Paul (in panel 20). (20) To the right of this same panel, S. Paul is addressing people (in panel 21). (21) Among those, Patroclus is seen falling. (22) He is taken up dead. (23) He comes back to life. (24) S. Paul and S. Peter baptising three men. (25) S. Paul and S. Peter before Nero. (26) Dogs jumping at them. (27) They seem to be praying to bring a dead man back to life (a modern panel). (28) S. Paul and S. Peter driving Simon the Magician out of a house. The man is all but naked and is worried by a dog (a modern panel). (29) The death of Simon. (30) Nero gives an order the two apostles should be put to death. (31) Plautilla gives S. Paul her veil. (32) The Saint is beheaded, and his eyes are bound with the veil. (33) He appears to Plautilla, and gives back the veil. (34, 35, 36) He appears to Nero in the middle panel. To the left, behind the saint, an angel with a censer. To the right, behind Nero, a man with a stick.

33. - THE STORY OF S. ANDREW

As in the preceding window, five rows are modern. — As the saint represented above had not been identifid when the chapel was restored in 1872, the painter chose to show, without any precise fact in view, apostles working out miracles or suffering martyrdom. A few panels are merely imitated from the old ones.

(1) Jesus giving S. Peter the keys. (2) S. Peter speaks to four barefooted men without halos. (3) S. Peter, between two women,

brings a dead man back to life (an imitation of panel 24). (4) S. Peter arrives at the gates of a town. (5) A saint is crucified on a horizontal cross (imitation of 29). (6) Jesus speaks to an apostle. (7) An apostle speaks to two men. (8) Two apostles pray, while idols fall. (9) An apostle sleeps on the ground (the figure is imitated from that in 21). (10) Jesus speaks to an apostle. (11) An apostle addresses a group of men. (12) A saint, who prays on his knees, is struck with clubs. (13) Two apostles conversing. (14) An apostle is led to death. (15) An apostle prays ; behind him, a man with a drawn sword.

The old panels all concern S. Andrew. For the clearness of the story, numbers 16 and 28 ; 18 and 23 should be interchanged.

(16) S. Andrew praying before his cross. In reality, this scene belongs to the third row starting from the top. (17) S. Andrew heals a blind man and gives him a red cloak. The meeting is in panel 28. (18) The apostle gives Holy Communion to a kneeling man. This is when he was in Philippi, after telling his disciples of his near death. (19, 20) He causes a serpent to die. Then he bids the proconsul's wife go and raise a child who had died from the serpent's bite. (21) He sees S. Peter and S. John in a dream, and is warned of his approaching death. (22) This panel must have belonged to the lower part of the window, and been one of a series recording the story of a young man wrongly charged with incest. Here the saint is walking before the young man, and will plead on his behalf. (23) He informs his disciples of his near death. The scene in panel 18 belongs here. (24) He brings a young man back to life. (25, 26) The proconsul orders the saint out of prison. (27) S. Andrew before the proconsul. (28) Explained already. (29) S. Andrew is bound on the cross. (30) The proconsul is reproached with the way he has treated the saint. (31) A repetition of scene 27. (32) The death of S. Andrew. (33) The punishment of the proconsul, who is tortured by a demon, and dies.

In the last row, Jesus between two angels holding censers.

34. - THE STORY OF THE APOSTLES

The scenes in this window are all taken from the gospels. (1, 2, 3) The bakers. (4-8) illustrate the gospel of S. John 1 35-40. (4) a modern panel, shows Jesus walking. In 5, John the Baptist says to his two disciples : Behold the Lamb of God ! In 6, the two disciples, one of whom is Andrew, follow Jesus. (7, 8) Jesus shows them where he dwells. (7 a modern panel) — (9) a modern panel, two apostles talk. (10) A modern panel, two men barefoot and without halos. (11) Jesus saying to Philip : Follow me. (12) A modern panel, two apostles looking at the preceding scene. (13) Jesus is sitting. Two apostles stand before him. These may be either Peter and Andrew or James and John. (14) Jesus in Simon's boat. (15) The boat of James and John. (16) Jesus lands. (17, 18) Jesus, followed by Peter and Andrew, calls James and John. The man who steers must de Zebedee. (19) Philip brings Nathanael to Jesus. (The inscription *Petrus* must have replaced an older one). (20) Apostles baptising — an allusion to John IV 2. (21) Nathanael under the fig-tree. (22) Christ conversing with his disciples. (23) A group of lookers-on. (24) A modern panel here shows again barefooted men without halos who seem to converse as they walk. (25) Jesus is speaking to his disciples of his Passion. (26) The Last Supper. (27) The washing of feet. (28) Jesus at the Mount of Olives. (29, 30) Armed men take hold of Jesus and strike him. The disciples forsake him. One of them is seen in the middle panel, thus connecting the two scenes. (31) Jesus, after his Resurrection, standing in the midst of his disciples. (32) He is carried up to heaven. (33) The descent of the Holy Ghost. (34) Christ blessing and holding the globe of the world.

35. - THE STORY OF SIMON AND JUDE

(1) The donor, Henry Noblet, is represented as a deacon praying before an image of the Virgin of Chartres. (2) The same donor, now a canon, is praying Christ himself. (3, 4) S. Simon and Jude, fellow-workers, are seen in Persia discussing with two magicians. (5, 6) A sacrifice offered to an idol ; another idol is consulted as to the issue of an expedition against invading Hindus. (7, 8) Simon and Jude, before general Warardac ; they pray that the idol, silent until then, may speak and prove its inefficiency. (9, 10) An idol is again consulted, while the apostles are revealing the issue of the expedition to Warardac. (11, 12) Two soothsayers are probably reporting against the apostles, who are imprisoned. (13, 14) Warardac sits in state awaiting the Hindu ambassadors (in accordance with what the apostles had foretold). (15, 16) The saints bid a new-born babe, the one to the right, deny as his father a man whom they had made a deacon. (17, 18) The magi of Persia making serpents, to vie

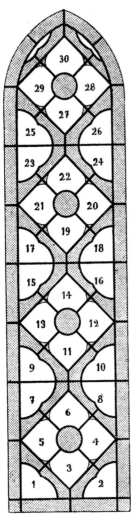

Saint James

with the miracles of the saints. The saints pray that the serpents may bite their authors without killing them utterly. (19, 20) The chariots of the Moon and Sun (which the saints refused to adore). (20, 21) formerly showed the martyrdom of the saints. The two angels are modern (1921).

36.

A grisaille of the thirteenth century,

37. - THE STORY OF S. JAMES THE GREATER

This and the next window are among the most beautiful in the church, both in colouring and design. — They are described in his usual amusing and informal way by Henry Adams : *Mont-Saint-Michel and Chartres* pp. 166-70.

For this window see the diagram. (1, 2) Furriers and drapers. (3) The saint receives the pilgrim's staff from Christ. (4) He preaches. (5) Almogines, the magician, inspired by a demon, is sending his disciple, Filetus, to dispute with James. (6) The meeting of S. James and Filetus. (7) Filetus telling Almogines of his conversion. (8) Filetus is bound by the magic of Almogines. (9) S. James sends his cloak to release Filetus. (10) A droll little demon leaves Filetus, crying like a child. (11) Almogines raises two demons to serve him. (12) The demons, who are bound and burned by infernal flames, beg the Saint's assistance. (13) They are sent to bind and bring back Almogines. (14) The meeting of Almogines, held by the demons, with S. James and Filetus. (15) The conversion of Almogines. (16) He is about to burn his books. (17) He throws them into the sea. (18) Almogines and Filetus kneel before S. James, begging forgiveness. (19) Almogines breaks the image he was wont to consult. (20) Almogines addressing his former adepts. (21) S. James is thrown into prison. (22) S. James addressing two men. (25) He is brought before Herod. (26) He is led away by a certain Josias, a Pharisee, and cures a paralytic. (24) The paralytic kneels before him. (23) Josias is struck down for declaring before the high priest that he is now a Christian. (27) S. James and Josias are led together. (28, 29) They are beheaded. (30) Christ on a cloud between two three-branched candlesticks.

38. - THE STORY OF CHARLEMAGNE

(1) Donors, the furriers.

Three episodes, connected with Charlemagne, are represented here. The first (2-7) deals with Emperor Constantine and the conquest of Jerusalem.

(2) Charlemagne between two bishops, the bringers of a letter from Constantine. (3) An angel has sent Constantine a vision in his sleep : he sees Charlemagne, Defender of the Faith, on horseback and in the full armour of the early thirteenth century. (4) Constantine welcomes Charlemagne at the gates of Constantinople. (5) The fight with the Saracens. — Note the heart-shaped shields of the French, and the round shields of the Infidels (6) Constantine gives Charlemagne three shrines containing relics, among which the *Sancta Camisia*, now the possession of the Church of Chartres. (7) Charlemagne presents them to the Church of Aix-la-Chapelle.

The second episode concerns Charlemagne's expedition to Spain. — (8) He looks up at the Milky Way. (9) The apparition of S. James the Major, who bids Charlemagne follow the Milky Way right into Spain and deliver his tomb from the Infidels. (10) Charlemagne on his way to Spain with Archbishop Turpin of Rheims. (11) Charlemagne, before his army, is praying for victory. (12) He takes Pampaluna. (13) He raises a church to S. James. (14) He fights a pagan king. (15) The so-called miracle of the lances. — The night before the battle, the soldiers who were to die had their lances flower as a symbol of martyrdom. (16) The combat of Roland with the giant Ferragus. (17) Ferragus is killed by Roland. (18) Charlemagne crossing the Pyrenees. (19) Roland is represented twice : splitting the rock with Durendal ; blowing his horn to call Charlemagne. (20) Roland dies, while Baudoin shows him no water can be found. (21) Baudoin has overtaken Charlemagne and apprises him of the sad news.

The last episode, one scene only, will be found in another window of the clerestory, and is also represented in the arch of the right bay (south porch). (22) The mass of S. Giles. — The saint is celebrating mass, an angel appears with a scroll on which the sin that Charlemagne did not confess is written. (28, 24) Two angels holding censers.

39. - THE STORY OF S. THEODORE AND S. VINCENT

To study this window, see the diagram, page 102.

(1, 2) The weavers, donors of the window. — The story of S. Theodore is told in the lower part of the window. That of S. Vincent is told in the panels above the signature. (3) S. Theodore, then a Roman soldier serving in Asia Minor, sets fire to a temple. (4) He is summoned before the judge. (5) He is put into prison. (6) Christ appears to him in the prison. (7) He is torn with rakes. (8) He is burnt alive. (9, 10) Two angels with censers.

(11) S. Vincent, a young Spanish nobleman, is made a deacon by the bishop of Saragossa. (12) He is summoned before a magistrate at Valencia. (13) He is put into prison. (14, 15) He is stripped of his garments and beaten in the presence of his judge. (16) The bishop of Saragossa is banished. (27) The judge condemns S. Vincent to be burnt on a gridiron (in the shape of a ladder). (28) S. Vincent is seen walking towards it. (25, 26) His martyrdom. (21) He is put into prison again. (22, 23) In his prison he converses with an angel. Two persons witness the miracle. (24) The magistrate is informed. (19, 20) Saint Vincent is released in the presence of the magistrate, who, inspired by a demon, intends to torture him again as soon as he has recovered. (17, 18) Bystanders. (29, 30) The Death of S. Vincent. (31) The corpse, which was left unburied, is protected by a raven. (32) Men telling the magistrate of this new miracle. (33) The magistrate giving

*The Charlemagne Window (13th Century)
Roland at Roncesvalles*

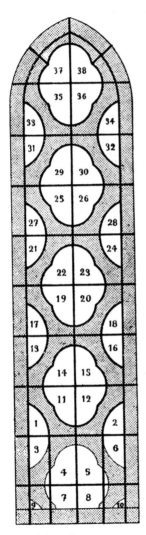

St Theodorus, St Vincent

orders. (34) The body is cast into the sea, with a millstone round its neck. (35, 36) The body, washed ashore, is tended by angels. (37, 38) The burial.

40. - THE STORY OF S. PANTALEON

(1) This window was given by a canon, whom we see kneeling before an image of the Virgin of Chartres. (2) Young Pantaleon is studying under a physician, in the ancient town of Nicomedia. (3) He is taught the Christian doctrine by a priest, Hermolaus. (4) He has brought back to life a young man, who had been bitten by a serpent (here a sort of dragon). (5) He is baptised. (6) He heals a blindman ; (7) then a paralytic. (8) He is brought to Maximian. (9) He is imprisoned. (10) He is fastened to a cross, and tortured. (11) Then he is placed in a pot of molten lead. (12) He is cast into the sea. (13) He is exposed to wild beasts, which do not harm him. (14) In his prison, he is visited by an angel. (16) He is tortured on the wheel. (16) This scene belongs to the same episode as panel 12. Christ walks on the waves to the rescue of the saint. (17, 18) S. Pantaleon is condemned and sent to be tortured. (19) The wheel breaks to pieces. (20) Maximian and another man witness the miracle. (21) S. Pantaleon is questioned by Maximian. (22) He comes for Hermolaus and his two companions. (23, 24) The four men pray in the presence of Maximian, while a messenger comes with the news the idols have fallen. (25, 26) The martyrdom and burial

of Hermolaus and his two companions. (27) A last interview. between Maximian and the Saint. (28) The saint prays while the executioners are getting their swords ready. (29) S. Pantaleon, tied to a tree, is about to be beheaded. (30) His body is burnt. — At the top of the window, we see his soul taken up to heaven by two angels, while, on either side, another angel is offering incense. Above, Christ blesses and holds the globe of the world.

41. - THE STORY OF S. STEPHEN
AND THE TRANSLATION OF HIS BODY

(1, 2) The shoemakers. On the right, they are seen at work. On the left, they offer a model of the window. (3) Stephen between two apostles. (4, 5) Stephen, disputes with Jews and confounds them. (6) He is brought before the Sanhedrin. (7) He sees the heavens opened. (8) He is cast out of the city. (9, 10) Witnesses lay down their clothes at the feet of Saul. Stephen is stoned : note the red glass of the head, to represent his wounds. (11) Devout men carrying him to his burial.

(12) Eight years later, a woman begs the patriarch of Jerusalem to let her take to Constantinople the body of her husband (who had erected a church to the memory of S. Stephen and had been buried near him). (13) The tomb is opened, disclosing two coffins. (14) The wife, with her husband's corpse, leaves Jerusalem, but she had mistakenly carried away the body of S. Stephen. (15) A demon appears to the king of an island, urging him to burn the vessel which carries the relics of the saint. (16) The king sends messengers to the shore. (17) The embarkment of the holy shrine. (18) Demons raise a tempest. (19, 20) The ship is nearing land, while a crowd has gathered on the shore. (21, 22) The body is carried to Constantinople, and the patriarch is walking out to meet it. (23) S. Stephen's soul is lifted up to heaven.

42. - THE STORY OF S. CHERON

(1, 2) Masons, stone-cutters and sculptors. — (3) S. Cheron, a young Roman, is brought to school. (4) He is at school. (5, 6) S. Cheron refuses to look at a young lady his parents wish him to marry. (7) Now a churchman, he heals a woman possessed of a devil. (8) He heals a blindman. (9) He addresses a group of disciples. (10) He heals a chariot-driver, victim of an accident. Note on the wheel a little demon, no doubt responsible for the mischief. (11) Near Chartres, he is assaulted by highwaymen. (12) He is beheaded, and then walks with his head in his hands, led by an angel while another censes him. (13) While two angels are about to carry his soul to heaven, the saint has reached the place of his burial (on the other side of the Eure, where a church and monastery were built afterwards). (14) The saint appears to the first abbot designating his tomb. (15, 16) The body is translated to another tomb, bishop Pappolus presiding over the ceremony. To the left, people cured by the the saint. (17-20) Two rows are concerned with the restoration to health of king Clothaire's son. First we see the king looking at his son. Then, near his tomb, S. Cheron appears to the young man and a priest, both bound on a pilgrimage to Tours. Above the latter scene, the young prince's escort is clearly off duty ; while, to the left, we see the pilgrims on their way back. (21-23) A short narrative concerning bishop Pappolus. On the left, we see a priest walking towards a town with a chalice lent by the bishop, but belonging to the monastery of S. Cheron. On the right, the bishop, who has been taken ill, is sending the chalice back to the abbey.

43. - THE STORY OF S. SAVINIAN
AND S. POTENTIAN, AND A WOMAN-MARTYR

This window had various donors. The second panel shows a mason at work. Higher up, in panels 17 and 18, we see first the congregation bringing their offerings, then weavers again as in the opposite window of the same chapel.

(1) Christ accepts the two saints as his disciples. The standing figure may be S. Peter himself. (3) They have followed S. Peter to Antioch, then to Rome. S. Peter is now sending them, together with Altinus, into Gaul. (4) They arrive in the surburbs of Sens. (5) They converse with citizens. (6) Two men are baptised. (7) S. Savinian, before entering Sens, marks the walls with a cross. He is already dressed as bishop. (8) The missionaries preaching. (9) S. Peter and S. Paul appear to S. Savinian. (10) Two saints stand before some man of authority. (11) S. Savinian and his companions baptise. A fourth saint has joined them. (12) The four saints are raising a church in Sens. (13) Five saints are standing near a town. (14) A bishop talking to two other saints. (15) S. Savinian and a disciple of his are condemned. (16) Their mar-

tyrdom. — Above the row occupied by the donors, we have quite another story. — (19) A woman brings food to three saints in prison. (20) Inside a lighted building (the crypt of the cathedral ?), she seems to pull a headless corpse out of a well. (21, 22) She is beheaded.

44.

This grisaille was placed here — and the stained glass taken out — in the middle of the thirteenth century.

45. - THE STORY OF S. JULIAN, THE HOSPITALIER

(1, 2, 3) Carpenters, joiners, cartwrights and coopers. (4) Julian's family. (5) Julian enters the household of a lord. (6) He waits on the lord and lady. (7, 8) He stands behind his lord who is dying. He receives a fee (represented by a sceptre). (9) The lord's death. (10) Julian's marriage. (11) The wedding feast. (12) He goes to war. (13) He is victorious. (14) He stands at the gate of a town or castle. (15) He sleeps in his tent. (The head is modern). (16) A servant brings his horse. (17) He arrives at the gate of his own castle. (18) He kills a woman and a man he finds sleeping together. (19) Then he meets his wife and is told he has killed his own parents. (20, 21) He mourns his parents (right panel). They are buried. (22) He goes away ; his wife insists on following him. (23) They embark. (24) They build a hospital near a river. (25) They welcome two travellers. (26) The saint's wife washes the feet of three travellers. (27) Christ, followed by an angel, appears to the saint, on the river-bank. (28, 29) His wife holds a light, while Julian ferries Christ across. (30) The death of both S. Julian and his wife.

46. - THE STORY OF OF S. THOMAS THE APOSTLE

See the diagram, page 106.

The bottom row is an old (thirteenth century) restoration. The fleur-de-lis of the right and left panels are not a signature. (1) S. Thomas touches the wound in Christ's side. (2) At Caesarea, Jesus informs Thomas he will have to go to India. (3) Jesus introduces his disciple to a messenger who has just landed from

Saint Thomas

India, and is looking for an architect. (4) Thomas sails away. (5) He lands at Andropolis. (6, 7) He feasts with the king and is struck by the chief butler who, having to go out for water, is devoured by a lion. Note the yellow dog that bites off the guilty hand and brings it back to the banquet hall. (8) In India, S. Thomas is introduced to the king. (9) The king gives him money for the building of a palace. (10) The king starts on a journey. (11, 12) Thomas spends the money on building churches and relieving the poor. (13) The king, returning, sends him to prison. (14) Gad, the king's brother, dies : his soul is received by an angel. (15) Gad, in heaven, is shown a curious building, the *Father's house with many mansions.* (16) The king, S. Thomas and Gad, who has been sent back to earth, converse. (16) The predication of S. Thomas : the king is converted (18, 19) In another part of the country, the saint suffers martyrdom. (20, 21, 22) He is brought before an idol (lower medallion). To the left, the idol falls while he is praying. To the right, the high priest stabs him. (23) The entombment of the saint. (24, 25) People — who are turned the wrong way about — look up at the tomb above them. (26) The tomb of the saint, with lamps burning, and sick people asleep, in memory of the miracles worked there. (27, 28) Angels with censers.

47, 48, 50, 51.

These four windows are thirteenth century grisailles. In the first, a stained glass medallion shows S. Lawrence on the gridiron.

In the oculi, Jesus surrounded first by angels, then by the four apocalyptic beasts.

53. - A MIRACLE OF S. NICHOLAS

The lower panels of this window as of the next are rather hard to study, being partly hidden by the wood-work of the chapel placed there at the beginning of the nineteenth century.

(1) Stephen Chardonel, a canon of Paris, donor of the window. (2) Members of his family. — The signature enables the historian to give 1242 as the latest possible date of this window.

The following scenes all refer to one miracle of the saint, when bishop of Myra. — (3) The Goddess Diana and worshippers. (4) S. Nicholas preaches. (5) He throws down the statue. (6) The devil appears to three magicians. (7, 8) The magicians prepare some malefic oil, called Midiacon. (15) The devil receives it at their hands. (10) This very dark panel seems to represent a person holding a phial. (11, 12) Boats sailing away to Myra. On the shore — to the right — the devil, in the shape of a woman, hands some passengers the liquor. (13, 14) A passenger throws something into the sea, no doubt in obedience to a command of S. Nicholas himself who appears in the second boat. (9, 16) The devout pilgrims reach Myra. (17, 18) S. Nicholas blesses them, before they return home.

54. - THE STORY
OF S. GERMAIN OF AUXERRE

(1) Donor : Geoffrey Chardonel, a canon of Chartres, and a relation of the Stephen in the twin window. As Geoffrey Chardonel died in 1236 the window must have been given and executed before that date. (2) S. Germain studying under a teacher. (3) The saint, chosen as the bishop of his native town, is brought away from home against his will. (4) His consecration. (5) A tax-collector begs the bishop to find the money he has lost (6) The bishop talking to a man possessed of a devil. (9) The bishop celebrates mass, while the devil comes out of the man possessed, and confesses the theft. (8) The thief giving back the money : the bishop blesses him. (9) A demon spreading a disease among the people. (10) S. Germain healing them. (11) S. Germain and S. Loup sailing to England : the devil raises a tempest. (12) S. Germain allaying the tempest. (13) S. Germain preaches in

England. (14) He heals a blind girl. (15, 16) A demon setting fire to the houses where S. Loup and S. Germain are lodged. (17) On his way to Italy, S. Germain has his horse stolen from him. (18) The thief restores the horse and is blessed by the saint. (19, 20) The saint is dying at Ravenna (right panel). His soul is taken up to heaven (left panel).

55.

In the oculus, Christ surrounded by the four apocalyptic beasts.

56.

The Peace Window.

Given by the German Association of Friends of Chartres Cathedral in 1971, and the work of the Chartres stained-glass window maker, François Lorin.

The principal themes of this window are those of Peace and Reconciliation, expressed in symbols taken from both the Old and New Testaments.

The window is made up of four super-imposed crosses, set against an ornamental background. In the centre of the lowest cross are the ten commandments, the basis of human salvation. To the left is the burning bush, a symbol for God's revelation to humanity through natural phenomena, and to the right is the seven-branched candlestick.

In the centre of the second cross is an altar and a rainbow, the symbol for God's covenant with Man. To the left, corn, and to the right, grapes, which give the eucharistic bread and wine, symbols chosen by Christ himself.

In the centre of the third cross there is a chalice set in a cruciform. To the left are seven flames symbolising the seven gifts of the Holy Spirit, and to the right, a sun. Christ said " I am the Light of the World ".

In the centre of the highest cross is the " Hand of God ", an ancient symbol for His divine power in the universe.

57.

The border of this window — except the left top panel — is old work and represents angels.

The thirteenth century glass filling the centre — the story of S. Lawrence — was taken out in 1791.

In 1924, pieces of 13th century glass from the choir, taken out and broken in the 18th century, were placed together here, and the modern glass is the work of Monsieur Lorin in 1967.

58. - THE PARABLE OF THE PRODIGAL SON

This window, without signature, illustrates the parable in S. Luke XV 11-12.

(1) The prodigal son asking for his portion goods. (2) The father gives him money and a precious vessel. (3) A servant or the elder son in the field. (4) The prodigal son journeying to a far country. (5, 6) He arrives at a city where he will waste his substance in riotous living. (7, 8, 9) He feasts with two courtesans. On either side, servants bring in dishes. (10) He lies on a bed and is tempted to gamble. (11) He is allured by courtesans. (12) He plays dice on a chessboard. (13) But he has lost, and is left with nothing but his hose. (14, 15) He begs. (16) He offers service to a citizen of that country. (17) He is herding swine. (18) He comes to himself and resolves to arise and go to his father. (19) He journeys home. (20) His father runs out to greet him. (21) A servant is bringing forth the best robe. (22) The fatted calf is being killed. (23) The kitchen, where every preparation is made for the feast. (24) The father, coming out to intreat the elder son. (25, 26, 27) The feast. The father is sitting with his two sons, and a servant is waiting on them. On the left, a fiddler playing. On the right, servants bring wine and a tankard. (28, 29, 30) Christ blesses the world between two worshipping angels.

59. - THE SYMBOLIC WINDOW

(1, 2, 3) The blacksmiths, as donors.

This is a symbolic window, in which the principal scenes of the Passion of Our Lord — represented in the four square panels in the centre — are surrounded with scenes of the Old Testament looked upon as figures or prototypes. — The seven top panels of the middle column are modern and were put in in 1923. They are very good imitations of similar scenes in Bourges, Le Mans and Canterbury.

Exceptionnally, this window must be read from top to bottom. See the diagram, page 110.

(4) Christ between two three-branched candlesticks. (5, 6, 7) Jesus bears his cross, between holy women and soldiers. In the original panel, Jesus walked to the right. (8) The two spies bringing back a bunch of grapes from Canaan. (9, 10) Jesus is crowned with thorns, and scourged. (11) Gideon visited by an angel while winnowing his corn. (12, 13, 14) Christ on the Cross between the Church and the Synagogue. (15) Adam receiving the blood of

Christ in a chalice (cf. window 18). (16, 17) Moses lifting up the brazen serpent. The elders of Israel striking the lintel with the blood of the passover. (18) Jonah probably fleeing from the presence of the Lord. (19, 20, 21) A Deposition, between two scenes of the sacrifice of Isaac. (22) David with a scroll on which was written quite plainly at one time the beginning of verse 6 of Psalm 102. Near him, the pelican, held in the Middle Ages to be a symbol of resurrection. (23, 24) Elisha followed by the Shunammite approaches the bed where her son is lying. Elijah at the gate of Zarephath meeting the widow who was gathering sticks. (25) Jacob blessing Ephraim and Manasseh, Joseph's sons, according to Gen. XLVIII 13-14. (26, 27, 28) The anointing of Christ's body, between Samson carrying off the gates of Gaza, and David among his sheep, slaying the lion.

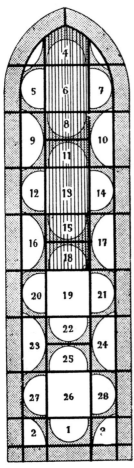

The Symbolic Window

60. - THE STORY AND MIRACLES OF S. NICHOLAS

This is the third window dealing with the life of S. Nicholas, and many scenes are the same as in window 27. — As the panels do not follow in satisfactory order, the diagram, must be consulted.

(1-5) Haberdashers and apothicaries. (6-7) Birth and bath of Nicholas. (8) He refuses to suckle his mother. (9) S. Nicholas in school. (10, 11) Still a young student in Myra, he drops money into a house for the three daughters' dowries. — The father is thanking him. (12) S. Nicholas is chosen as the new bishop. (13) His consecration. (14, 15) The unloading of corn. (16, 17) The corn is distributed. (18, 19) The three young men welcomed and killed by an innkeeper. (20) A woman outside a door. Inside, a child is having his bath in a tub placed over the fire. This scene does not seem connected to any other. (21, 22) The story of the child who fell into the sea. (23-25) The story of the Jew and the dishonest Christian. (26) A man is striking the statue of the saint who did not protect him from robbers.

61. - THE STORY OF JOSEPH

(1, 2) The bankers. — The window tells the story of Joseph : Genesis XXXVII, XXXIX-XLVI. (3) The second dream of Joseph, when he sees the sun and the moon and the eleven stars making obeisance to him. (4) Jacob sends him to his brothers. (5) The brothers conspire against him. (6, 7, 8) In the middle, he is cast into a pit. To the left, he is sold to Ishmaelite merchants. To the right, the brothers bring Jacob Joseph's coat of many colours. (9, 10, 11) In Egypt, Joseph is sold to Potiphar. He is tempted by Potiphar's wife. She accuses him. (12, 13) Potiphar has him arrested. Joseph is thrown into prison. (The heads of Pharaoh's butler and baker are seen rising above the prisonwall.) (14, 15, 16) In the centre, Pharaoh is sleeping. His dream of the seven fatfleshed and the seven leanfleshed kine is shown on the left. On the right, Joseph interprets the dreams of the butler and baker. (17, 18, 19) He interprets Pharaoh's dream.

The Egyptians sow corn, and then store their grain during the seven plenteous years. (20,21) Jacob sends his sons to buy corn from Egypt. The sons on their journey. (In this and in three other panels, note how well drawn the camels are.) (22, 23, 24) Joseph, as governor of the land, welcomes his brothers. — The brothers (on their second journey) eating in

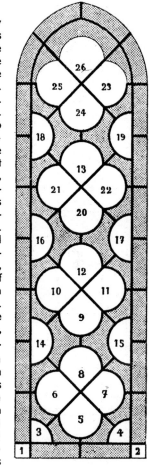

Saint Nicholas

Joseph's house. — On their way back, the cup of Joseph is found in Benjamin's sack. (25, 26, 27) Jacob walks out to meet his sons, whose procession with camels and asses fills the two other panels. (28, 29) Jacob and his sons on their way to Egypt. The meeting of Jacob and Joseph. (30) Christ blessing.

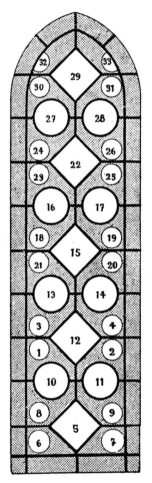

Saint Eustace

62. - THE STORY OF S. EUSTACE

The donors are the drapers. (1, 2), and the furriers (3, 4). (5) Placidas hunting the stag. (6-9) Around him, huntsmen and hounds. (10) The conversion of Placidas. (He sees the crucifix between the antlers of the stag.) (11) He is baptised as Eustace. (12) He leaves the city with his wife and two children. (13, 14) He bargains with a shipmaster. They all embark for Egypt. (15) The shipmaster drives the children and Eustace out of the ship, and detains the wife. (16, 17) While Eustace is fording the river between his two sons, a pink lion is carrying one off, and a wolf, which has seized the other, is attacked by shepherds. (18, 19) Emperor Trajan sends for Placidas. The emissaries lodge with Eustace. (20, 21) They converse in his house. — The two children, soldiers under their father, discover they are brothers. (22) The recognition of Eustace, a general again, and his wife in India. (23) Two young recruits (who are his own sons) are brought to Eustace. (24) The wife going to ask a favour from the Roman general. (25) The family are reunited and feasting. (26) The meaning of this little scene is not known. (27, 28) Hadrian kneeling before Appolo in thanksgiving. Eustace is brought to the temple. (29) Eustace and his family are burnt in a brazen bull. A hand from heaven confers the crown of martyrdom. (30-33) A magistrate and other men, witnessing the scene. A man brings fresh wood to the fire.

63. - THE STORY OF S. LUBIN

See the diagram.

The wine-merchants, donors of the window, are represented in twenty-three medallions. — The medallion that is numbered 24 shows the highest use to which wine can be put, in the Eucharist. Above that (25), Christ blesses, holding a book with the letters Alpha and Omega.

The story of S. Lubin, a shepherd-boy of Poitiers who became a bishop of Chartres in the sixth century, is told in the medallions to right and left. — (26, 27) These panels are not understood. (28, 29) Young Lubin grazing his sheep. A monk is writing the alphabet on the young man's belt. (20, 31) Lubin's father is procuring him a regular alphabet. The youth is studying while his companion drinks. (32, 33) Lubin entering a monastery ; then welcoming visitors. (34, 35) He travels with two other monks. (36, 37) They reach the monastery of S. Avit in Perche. S. Lubin is appointed cellarer and given the keys. (38, 39) He is consecrated as bishop of Chartres. He sets out to visit his diocese. (40, 41) Three men being present, the bishop makes holy water to sprinkle over a house infested with demons.

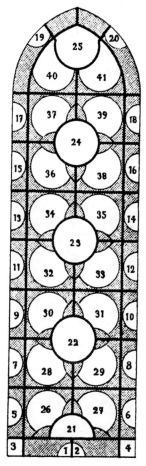

Saint Lubin

64. - THE STORY OF NOAH

See the diagram. (1-5) The coopers, carpenters and wheel-wrights. (6-9) These medallions are very difficult to undertand. The begins the story of Noah as it is given in Gen. VI-IX. — First the Flood.

Noah

(10) God speaking to Noah. (11) Noah builds the ark. (12, 13) Men and women (perhaps Noah's sons, wife and daughters-in-law) watch the proceedings. (14) A man and a woman seem to be walking away from the ark. (15-18) The animals, two of every sort, come to the ark. Note the birds flying aloft. (19) The ark floats upon the waters. (24) Noah sends forth the dove out of the ark. (25) The dove is seen flying away, then returning with an olive leaf in its mouth. (20-23, 26, 27) Men destroyed from the earth. The flood recedes, and the animals leave the ark. (29) A raven devours corpses. (30, 31) Animals are seen walking away. The next panels are concerned with Noah's making wine. — (32) The discovery of the vine. (33) Three men at work in the vineyard planted by Noah. (34) Noak makes wine. (35) Noah, in his tent, is drinking of the wine. (36) He curses Ham, who witnessed his drunkenness.

The top of the window reminds us of the covenant established between God and man. — (37) God is speaking from above the rainbow : Noah and his wife listen on their knees. (38) The rest of the family, in the same attitude. Four panels (39-42) contain angels swinging censers.

The Upper Storey

The windows of the upper storey

mostly represent tall figures of prophets, apostles and saints, with, here and there, a few scriptural or legendary subjects. With exception of the apse and ends of the transept, each bay has two windows surmounted by a rose 5 ms 50 in diameter.

The windows will be described in the same order as before, starting from the south tower.

65. - S. Mary the Egyptian. In the lower panels, she meets with Zozimus ; she is buried.

66. - S. Laumer, abbot of Corbion. Below, he is seen lying on his death-bed and visited by S. Malard.

67. - In the rose, an abbot.

68. - S. James the Major. Donors, the bakers and pastrycooks.

69. - S. Peter. Donors, the bakers.

70. - In the rose, Christ sitting between Alpha and Omega.

71. - The Virgin standing with the Child on her left arm, one breast uncovered. Below her, a *Noli me tangere* scene.

72. - S. Foy. Below, she is on the gridiron.

73. - In the rose, S. Solennis, a bishop of Chartres.

74. - S. James the Major. Below, a family as donors of the window.

75. - S. Philip and Jeremiah.

76. - In the rose, S. Jerome, a Doctor of the Church.

77. - S. Caletric. The signature is that of the turners.

78. - (party hidden by the organ). — S. Bartholomew and Moses. Same donors.

79. - In the rose, S. Augustine.

80, 81. - The windows were walled in at an unknown date, the organ being already there.

82. - In the rose, S. Gregory the Great.

83. - (partly hidden by the organ). — Two unknown saintly women.

84. - S. Symphorian, with his martyrdom below. Much of this window is modern.

85. - In the rose, S. Hilary (the bishop of Poitiers).

86, 87. - S. Peter and S. Paul.

88. - In the rose, Jean de Courville, a deacon, as donor of the three windows.

89. - S. Anthony with an unknown saint.

90. - A modern window (1928).

91. - In the rose, the donor, an ecclesiastic standing before an altar.

92. - Prophet Micah. Donor, Alix de Thouars, wife to Pierre Mauclerc.

93. - Prophet Malachi above Pierre Mauclerc's coat of arms.

94. - In the rose, Pierre Mauclerc on horseback and in full armour.

95. - The South Rose, glorifies Christ. according to the Book of Revelation. — In the centre, Christ sits enthroned, surrounded by angels together with the four beasts and, in the outer circles, by the twenty-four Elders of the Apocalypse.

Under the rose, five lancet windows. In the centre (A), Mary stands with the Child on her left arm ; and, by her side, the four major prophets, tawny and grim, carry the four evangelists astride their shoulders. No more striking symbol could have been chosen to show how the Old Covenant is the permanent foundation, of which the New is the fulfilment. S. Matthew (B) sits on Isaiah ; S. Luke (C) on Jeremiah ; S. John (D) on Ezekiel ; S. Mark (E) on Daniel. — Under these, the family of the donors. In the centre, the arms of Dreux-Brittany (chequers and ermines) ; to the right, Pierre Mauclerc and his son ; to the left, his wife and little daughter.

96. - Prophet Hosea. Under him, the same coat of arms.

97. - A prophet. Donor, Pierre Mauclerc.

98. - In the rose, a seated Virgin with the Child standing on her left knee.

99. - S. Come and S. Damian. Below, a priest, named Geoffrey, stands before an altar.

100. - S. Gervais and S. Protais. Perhaps the same donor.

101. - In the rose, the Virgin is seated, holding the Child on her left arm, between an angel and a lady donor.

102. - A knight of the Clement family receives the oriflamme from S. Denis himself. His coat of arms fills the lowest medallion.

103. - Two unknown saints. Donor, the same Geoffrey as before.

104. - In the rose, John the Baptist.

105. - The Nativity, the Flight to Egypt. Donor, *Colinus de camera*

regis playing chess with another man. — Notice all the borders in the choir are modern.

106. - S. John the Evangelist and S. James the Greater ; above, the adoration of the Magi. Donor, Bouchard de Marly, with his coat of arms.

107. - In the rose, a knight-in-armour beginning the procession of seven kings or high lords we see on either side of the

Ezechiel and Saint John

The Virgin

Isaïah and Saint Matthew

choir, leading towards the sanctuary. Here we have a member of the Beaumont family, belonging to the neighbourhood of Chartres.

108, 109. - These windows were taken out in 1788. They told, respectively, the stories of S. George and S. Eustace. Two panels at the bottom of window 108 show, in the one, a few spokes of the wheel on which S. George was tortured ; in the other, the fire under the brazen bull. Modern grisailles now fill in the windows.

110. - In the rose, a knight of the Courtenay family.

111. - A colossal figure of S. Paul. Donors, the curriers.

112. - An episode of the story of S. Vincent. See n° 39. Donor, a deacon called *Petrus Baillart*.

113. - In the rose, a knight of the Montfort family.

114, 115. - The stained glass windows were taken out in 1773. The present grisailles are modern.

116. - In the rose, a knight of the Montfort family, as before.

117. - Donors, the bankers. The Annunciation to Zacharias in the temple. John the Baptist bearing testimony to Jesus as the Lamb of God. The Baptism of Jesus.

118. - Donors, the clothiers. Daniel, Jeremiah, a Cherub.

119. - Donors, the bakers. Moses and the burning bush. Isaiah. An angel swinging a censer.

120. - Central window. — Donors, the bakers. Annunciation. Visitation. Mary as Queen, with the Child in her lap.

121. - Donor : a certain Geoffrey, a hosier, with his wife and two children. Aaron. A tall angel swinging a censer.

122. - Donors, the butchers. Ezechiel, Daniel and a Cherub.

123. - Donors, the bankers again. S. Peter is given the keys. He goes out of prison. He meets Jesus.

124, 125. - The windows were taken out in 1773. The grisailles are modern.

126. - In the rose, the Dauphin Louis, who was to become king Louis VIII.

127. - This window and the next relate episodes from the life of S. Martin. Here, we have the story of the cloak and the beggar (See n° XXIV) Donor, Thibault VI, Count of Chartres.

128. - S. Martin brings a dead man back to life and heals a dumb woman. Same donor.

129. - In the rose, the same donor again.

130, 131. - The stained glass windows were taken out in 1788. The grisailles are modern.

132. - In the rose, a king of Castille.

133. - Two groups of peasant-pilgrims. Below, the donor : Robert de Bérou, a chancellor of the cathedral.

134. - The Virgin, a tall seated figure, with the Child in her lap. The coat of arms figured in the medallion below, indicates the donor was a relation of Regnault de Mouçon, a bishop of Chartres, who died in 1217.

135. - In the rose, Jesus sitting between two three-branched candlesticks.

136. - The Annunciation, Nativity, Adoration of the Magi. Donor, the wife of the gentleman in the next window.

137. - S. Eustace (1) meeting the stag, (2) being baptized, (3) brought before an idol. Donor, a knight of another Beaumont family, near the river Oise.

138. - In the rose, Christ seated between the Sun and moon, blesses and holds the globe of the world.

139, 140. - These two windows are the exact counterpart one of the other, and were executed from the same design. They represent, respectively, S. Philip and S. Jude ; S. Andrew and S. Philip. Donor, an unknown priest kneeling before an altar on which is a chalice.

141. - In the rose, the same donor.

142. - S. Thomas and S. Jude. Below, again an unknown priest.

143. - S. Thomas and S. Barnaby. Same signature.

144. - In the rose, Christ as in n° 138.

145. - The North Rose. This rose, the *Rose of France* of Henry

Virgin and Child
(13th Century)

119

Adams, is given to the glorification of the Virgin, surrounded with figures of the Old Testament. Inside the church therefore, two roses at both ends of the transept emphasize the very same idea which is expressed in the porches. — The Virgin sits in the centre with the Child in her lap. In a circle around her, four doves, four angels and four Thrones are represented. In the outer circles, we find in succession the twelve kings of Judah, who were Mary's ancestors, and the twelve minor prophets.

Under the rose, five lancets. In the central lancet (A), S. Anne with the infant Virgin on her left arm ; then (B) David and Saul, the latter killing himself, his body pierced with a sword ; (C) Melchizedeck, with Nebuchadnezzar beneath him ; (D) Solomon with Jeroboam worshipping two calves ; and finally (E) Aaron above Pharaoh covered by the waters of the Red Sea. — Under S. Anne, a shield with the arms of France. In eight little windows in the corners below the rose are seen alternately the arms of France and Castille. The date therefore must be the time when Queen Blanche was regent (c. 1230).

146, 147, 148. - The windows and rose are thirteenth century grisailles showing the lilies of France and the castles of Castille in the borders.

149. - The legend of Joachim and Anne : the twofold Annunciation ; the meeting at the Golden Gate. This window though modern, reproduces the original subject. — At the bottom, Jane, Philip Boarskin's daughter is shown as the donor of the window. But, while the ancient glass represented a little girl, the modern panel is a mere copy of her mother, in the next window.

150. - The Annunciation and Visitation. Donor, Mahaut of Boulogne, Philip's wife.

151. - In the rose, which is modern, S. Anne holds the infant Virgin.

152. - The Angels appear to the shepherds. The Presentation in the Temple. Angels with censers. At the bottom, Philip Boarskin, Count of Boulogne and an uncle of S. Louis, is represented kneeling before an altar.

153. - The Death, Assumption and Coronation of the Virgin. Below, the shield of Philip Boarskin, which bears the blason of France.

154. - In the rose, Philip dressed in armour, on a white horse.

155. - The legend of S. Martin again. This window was offered by the citizens of Tours.

156. - An unknown person (the bust and head are modern). S. Martin. Same donors.

157. - In the rose, a man and his wife, kneeling on either side of a Virgin of Chartres, represent a whole group of donors.

158. - Abraham about to sacrifice Isaac. Below, the ram. Above, Jesus between Alpha and Omega.

159. - Jesus, a standing figure, clad in white. Under him, the sacrifice of Isaac again.

160. - In the rose, ploughmen as donors.

161. - S. George in the garb of an Oriental warrior, with his martyrdom below.

162. - S. Giles. In the medallion below, S. Giles' mass. See 38, top-panel.

163. - In the rose, S. George on horseback crushes a dragon.

164. - An apostle and the signature of the bankers.

165. - Six apostles.

166. - In the rose, the Virgin Mary as a *Sedes Sapientiae*. On the right and left, the six other gifts of the Holy Spirit are shown radiating from the central figure of Christ.

167. - S. Nicholas, given by the curriers.

168. - Four apostles, with the furriers as donors.

169. - In the rose, S. Thomas of Canterbury.

170. - S. Stephen. Below him, his martyrdom and the signature of the weavers.

171. - S. Lawrence. His martyrdom.

172. - In the rose, bishop S. Lubin.

173. - Three prophets : Jonah, Daniel, Habakkuk.

174. - The three temptations of Christ.

175. - In the rose, a holy bishop.

176. - The West Rose. We have come back to the western front to study the rose above the twelfth century lancets. — More subdued in colour, more severe also in its quiet majesty, it portays the Last Judgment. Christ sits in the centre, showing his five wounds, surrounded by the four beasts and angels. To right and left the twelve apostles sit, while above and below are Abraham with the elect and the weighing of the souls. In the outer circle we have in pairs, the scenes being perfectly balanced to right and left : the

instruments of the Passion, at the top ; then, working down, angels blowing the last trumpet ; resurrected men awaiting the sentence ; the dead rising from their tombs (four medallions) ; hell.

This brief description is entirely based on the full description — preceded by a history of the windows — given by Canon Delaporte in his monograph " *Les Vitraux de la Cathédrale de Chartres* ", published together with three volumes of plates by Mr. Houvet, the well-known custodian.

The visitor may be interested to know that the windows were taken out during both wars, and gradually put back after having been cleaned, releaded, and repaired when necessary.

Signature of the Furriers, donors
(13th Century)
(see window n° 37)

The Holy Trinity (14th Century)

THE SAINT PIAT CHAPEL
IT'S GLASS
AND THE CATHEDRAL TREASURE

Even in a short study, we must distinguish from the rest the two windows of the bay next the door as being more recent work. The older glass belongs to the fourteenth century.

Apsidal window

This window has six lights, and the head is a very good example of French decorated tracery. — In the lower part, six figures of saints are surmounted by canopies of a religious or military character alternately. With two exceptions, the figures may be identified by an inscription. From left to right are : (1) S. Turiaf, a bishop of Dol, in Brittany ; (2) S. Thecla, a woman-martyr ;

(3) S. Piat ; (4) S. Tugdual, a bishop of Tréguier, again in Brittany ; he is seen wearing the conic tiara, according to an erroneous belief he had been a pope. (5), (6) either S. Luqin, S. Caletric, S. Bethaire, or S. Solennis, all bishops of Chartres who, at the time, had some of their relics in Chartres together with the other saints represented in this window.

The head of the window shows a Last Judgment.

Virgin (14th Century)

Lateral windows

The two next windows on the right and left are smaller in size, and more sober in their decoration. Out of the three panels that make up the lights, the central ones only are filled with figures. Above and below are grisaille panels relieved by coloured borders. In the tracery, consisting mainly of three qua-trefoils, grisaille and colour are harmo-niously combined. — With one excep-tion, we must notice the individual cha-racter of the decoration. Not only has each window its own border, but a spe-cial pattern is represented on the gri-saille ground as well of the head as of the lights.

First window on the right (near the apse).

In the head, an image of the Trinity, under which two angels are swinging censers.

In the lights, a Virgin between two angels (one of whom is modern).

Second window.

In the head a Crucifixion, with the Virgin and S. John. In the two other qua-trefoils, the man who gave Jesus a sponge filled with vinegar and the soldier who pierced his side with a spear. — The scene is quite different in spirit from that of the twelfth and thirteenth centuries.

Below, two executioners are stoning S. Stephen (who is modern).

First window on the left (near the apse).

In the head, the mystic Lamb.

In the lights, an Annunciation, much of which is modern.

Second window. —

In the head, an image of S. Piat (modern), and charming little angels.

In the lights, S. Dionysius the Aeropagite and S. Lawrence.

First bay

The architecture of the windows is the same as in the older bays. The glass is sixteenth century work.

Right window : mostly grisaille.

Left window. — In the head, S. Mary Magdalene lifted up by angels. Below her, the Virgin and Child, and the Virgin welcomed in Heaven.

To the lower lights belong a figure of the Virgin and a donor that show an evolution in the technique of stained glass. Indeed this is more like a painting in oil than the decoration of a window.

Below, four charming little figures of liberal arts · *Geometry Arithmetic, Dialectic, Rhetoric,* placed there at an unknown date, but no doubt originally intended for some other window.

The treasure is exhibited here in the Saint Piat Chapel. It's most important possession is the so-called Veil of the Virgin (except on Sundays when it is placed on the altar of Notre-Dame-du-Pilier) Also on exhibit are liturgical vestments, ex-votoes, and several sculptured scenes from the old roodscreen, built during the reign of Saint Louis, and demolished in the 18th century.

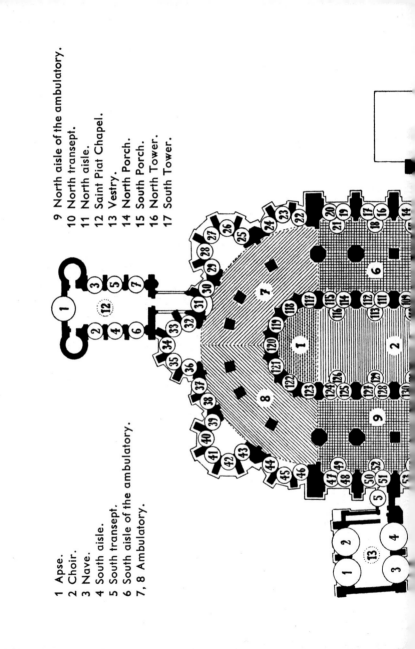

1 Apse.
2 Choir.
3 Nave.
4 South aisle.
5 South transept.
6 South aisle of the ambulatory.
7, 8 Ambulatory.

9 North aisle of the ambulatory.
10 North transept.
11 North aisle.
12 Saint Piat Chapel.
13 Vestry.
14 North Porch.
15 South Porch.
16 North Tower.
17 South Tower.

Le Corbusier 1926

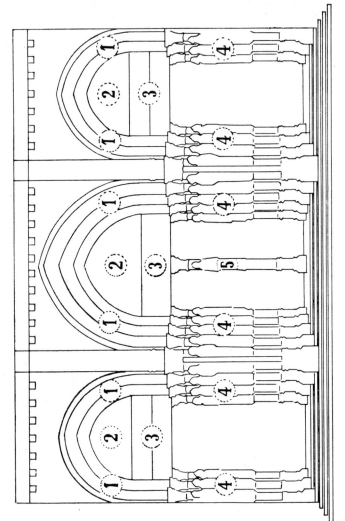

1 Archivolts
2 Tympanum
3 Lintel
4 Jambs